ASIA SMALL AND MEDIUM-SIZED ENTERPRISE MONITOR 2020

VOLUME IV—TECHNICAL NOTE: DESIGNING A SMALL AND MEDIUM-SIZED ENTERPRISE DEVELOPMENT INDEX

DECEMBER 2020

ASIAN DEVELOPMENT BANK

ADB

Contents

Tables, Figures, and Boxes

Foreword

Countries across developing Asia have taken several measures over the past decades to promote the development of micro, small, and medium-sized enterprises (MSMEs). Although governments have helped MSMEs improve market access, develop entrepreneurship, adopt technology, and access finance regularly, constraints on MSME development remain in most countries.

This report—Volume IV of the Asia Small and Medium-Sized Enterprise Monitor (ASM) 2020—is a technical note for designing a new, empirically rigorous cross-country index called the Small and Medium-Sized Enterprise Development Index (SME-DI). It aims to capture the structural problems MSMEs face, and measures the level of MSME development and access to finance using multivariate analytical methods based on national MSME data. The data are collected through ASM research and firm-level granular data obtained with consent to construct the SME-DI. It offers more insight and evidence to guide policymakers in the region.

The SME-DI is an ambitious but challenging initiative—as available MSME data remain limited and firm-level data are generally confidential and publicly unavailable. For a first step in building the SME-DI, this report develops a framework design for a feasible SME-DI. It also test-runs a pilot index (selected dimensions) for Southeast Asia and discusses challenges in developing the index.

For the test-run, we used two sets of data—aggregate MSME data captured by the ASM 2020 with time series and granular enterprise data that Credit Bureau Cambodia granted us to use to design the SME-DI. This report does not intend to develop a complete index at this stage, but rather raises issues in designing the index through the pilot exercise. The study will continue in 2021. Thus, we would appreciate it if readers could provide us with comments and suggestions to further develop the SME-DI for developing Asia.

Yasuyuki Sawada
Chief Economist and Director General
Economic Research and Regional Cooperation Department
Asian Development Bank

Acknowledgments

The Asia Small and Medium-Sized Enterprise Monitor (ASM) 2020 Volume IV was prepared by Shigehiro Shinozaki, senior economist, Economic Research and Regional Cooperation Department (ERCD) of the Asian Development Bank (ADB); and Mike Troilo, ADB consultant and associate professor of international business and finance, Collins College of Business, University of Tulsa, United States. The work was supervised by Joseph Ernest Zveglich Jr., deputy chief economist. It benefitted from inputs by Masato Abe, economic affairs officer at the Macroeconomic Policy and Financing for Development Division of the United Nations Economic and Social Commission for Asia and the Pacific (ESCAP), Thailand; and Phanhpakit Onphanhdala, deputy director of the Center for Enterprise Development and International Integration Policy, National Institute for Economic Research, Lao People's Democratic Republic.

The country pilot Small and Medium-Sized Enterprise Index (SME-DI) exercise was conducted in cooperation with the Credit Bureau Cambodia (CBC) team that included Sothearoath Oeur, chief executive officer of CBC; Huon Lida; and Vanndy Vat. We very much appreciate their active support for data compilation in designing the country pilot SME-DI despite their busy workloads. The study was carried out throughout 2020. Administrative support was provided by Richard Supangan and Maria Frederika Bautista.

Abbreviations

ADB	—	Asian Development Bank
AIIT	—	Advanced Institute of Industrial Technology (Japan)
APEN	—	Asia Professional Education Network
ASEAN	—	Association of Southeast Asian Nations
ASM	—	Asia Small and Medium-Sized Enterprise Monitor
CBC	—	Credit Bureau Cambodia
CIES	—	Cambodia Inter-censal Economic Survey
CIS	—	Credibility Index for SMEs
COVID-19	—	coronavirus disease
DFM	—	dynamic factor modeling
ERCD	—	Economic Research and Regional Cooperation Department
ERIA	—	Economic Research Institute for ASEAN and East Asia
FCI	—	financial conditions index
GDP	—	gross domestic product
IFC	—	International Finance Corporation
IMF	—	International Monetary Fund
ITC	—	International Trade Centre
KOF	—	Konjunkturforschungsstelle (Swiss economic institute)
LPI	—	Logistics Performance Index
MFI	—	microfinance institution
MSME	—	micro, small, and medium-sized enterprise
NBFI	—	nonbank finance institution
NPL	—	nonperforming loan
OECD	—	Organisation for Economic Co-operation and Development
OLS	—	ordinary least squares
PCA	—	principal component analysis
PCP	—	principal component pursuit
PRC	—	People's Republic of China
SME-DI	—	Small and Medium-Sized Enterprise Development Index

Executive Summary

In developing Asia, micro, small, and medium-sized enterprises (MSMEs) stimulate domestic demand, job creation, innovation, and competition; they are the backbone of national economies. MSME development is a policy priority as it accelerates inclusive growth across the region. Developing Asian countries have taken several measures to promote MSME development over the past decades—including support for market access, entrepreneurships, technology adoption and commercialization, and providing regular access to finance. However, MSMEs face formidable business constraints in most countries despite these government interventions.

A solid evaluation of MSME policies, based on real data, has yet to be conducted nationally and regionally due to limited data availability and comparability. To capture the structural problems affecting MSMEs, this report examines the feasible design of a new cross-country index we call the Small and Medium-Sized Enterprise Development Index (SME-DI). It aims to numerically measure the level of MSME development and access to finance using multivariate analytical methods. Measurements are based on national MSME data collected through the Asia SME Monitor (ASM) project and firm-level data obtained with consent from providers.

The SME-DI is an ambitious but challenging initiative—as available MSME data remain limited and firm-level data are generally confidential and publicly unavailable. As a first step, this report developed a framework design for a feasible SME-DI and conducted a test-run of a pilot index (selected dimensions) for Southeast Asia. We also discuss the challenges we encountered in developing the index. The report does not intend to present a complete index at this stage, but raises issues in constructing the index using the pilot exercise.

There are several stages in developing an index that measures specific aspects of MSMEs and policy interventions in Asia. Ongoing global and regional MSME data initiatives—led by Asian Development Bank (ADB), Asia Professional Education Network, Economic Research Institute for ASEAN and East Asia, International Finance Corporation, International Trade Centre, Organisation for Economic Co-operation and Development, and World Bank—include a thematic study and a country-level data analysis. ADB's SME-DI and other existing MSME indexes are similar in terms of analytical dimensions but not in methodology; the scoring and weighting are qualitative in existing indexes, while the SME-DI utilizes a more quantitative approach for both cross-sectional and panel data.

The SME-DI builds upon several composite indexes published over the past decade that capture various economic outcomes globally and in the Asia and Pacific region. After a review of index development, the study examines a two-stage principal component analysis (PCA) to estimate weights of selected variables and normalize different indicators—to create a composite index. In case of limited sample size and/or possible impact of outliers, the study considers other analytical approaches—such as dynamic factor modeling (DFM) and principal component pursuit (PCP)—and then chooses the most optimal method for the initial quantitative analysis.

Two sets of data were used for the test-run of the two-stage PCA: (i) aggregate MSME data captured by the ASM 2020 for the regional SME-DI and (ii) granular company data in Cambodia that Credit Bureau Cambodia (CBC) allowed us to use to design the country SME-DI.

By using aggregate MSME data, the pilot regional SME-DI was estimated using three dimensions (Macro, Bank, Nonbank) and four dimensions (the prior three plus Equity). The former is more plausible given data availability, while the latter we will flesh out later given the importance of equity financing. The estimates show that macro conditions are most significant in MSME development. Meanwhile, MSME financing remains important, where the weights for Bank and Nonbank are almost equal. Policymakers need to pay attention to both financing sectors, though their approach to each will likely differ. Access to bank credit may require more financial literacy training for MSMEs, so as to increase their success rate for obtaining bank loans. On the other hand, MSMEs generally find it easier to access finance from nonbank finance institutions, so further developing this sector makes sense.

The second analysis yielded the initial findings from a test-run of the two-stage PCA, based on CBC administrative enterprise data only. The result shows the estimated scores of the financial depth dimension under the Finance Sub-Index at the national level. In terms of financial access, products, and soundness, the result suggests that loans from state-owned banks and US dollar (USD)-denominated loans from private banks—with real estate security and corporate guarantees—positively affect MSME financial depth, thus supporting their access to investment capital finance. Financing MSMEs holds relatively higher risk than financing large firms. The nonbank finance industry represented by MFIs contributed relatively less to MSME access to finance, suggesting more diversified financing options for MSMEs. To increase the financial depth of MSMEs, more structured risk management for MSME loans is required with a rethinking of the role played by state-owned banks.

Notable challenges to the SME-DI design were data availability and consistency. Southeast Asia has relatively better data availability on MSMEs than other regions within developing Asia. Nevertheless, more data are needed to correctly estimate an SME-DI. Further efforts are required to obtain country data through (i) extended data-sharing agreements with public and private sector institutions that hold MSME data, including statistics offices, business registration offices, credit bureaus, government authorities, financial authorities, and central banks; and (ii) dedicated national firm-level surveys to collect missing data.

Going forward, the MSME database should be further strengthened through the ASM project with necessary stakeholder surveys. Using more granular firm-level data should be encouraged by strengthening data-sharing agreements with MSME data-holding institutions. For the next step, other analytical options such as DFM and PCP should be tested, with supplementary analysis using regression models and qualitative scoring methods. This study will continue to test these.

Introduction

In developing Asia, micro, small, and medium-sized enterprises (MSMEs) are the backbone of national economies. They stimulate domestic demand, create jobs, and drive innovation and competition. Thus, MSME development is a key policy for promoting inclusive growth in the region. Developing Asian countries have taken several measures to promote MSME development over the past decades—supporting market access, developing entrepreneurship, adopting technology and commercialization, and accessing finance regularly. However, business constraints facing MSMEs remain formidable in most countries despite government intervention.

More critically, MSMEs in developing Asia face the highest financing gap in the world. According to the International Finance Corporation report (2017), the Asia and Pacific region[1] accounted for 52% of the global MSME financing gap, or $2.7 trillion. Women-led MSMEs have great difficulty in accessing finance, estimated at $1.4 trillion in the region, or 83% of the global total. Government measures such as public credit guarantees and secured lending legal reforms have yet to tangibly contribute to reducing the MSME financing gap.

A solid evaluation of MSME policies, based on real data, has yet to be sufficiently conducted at the national and regional levels in developing Asia. This is due to limited data availability and comparability. To capture the structural problems surrounding MSMEs with evidence, this report constructs a new cross-country index called the Small and Medium-Sized Enterprise Development Index (SME-DI).[2] It numerically measures the level of MSME development and access to finance using multivariate analytical methods based on national MSME data. These are collected through the Asia SME Monitor (ASM) project and firm-level data from Asian countries given us to construct the SME-DI. It will help government authorities identify comparative strengths and weaknesses of policy interventions on MSME development and access to finance nationally, and design evidence-based policymaking for these areas.

The conceptual framework for the SME-DI comprises two subindexes: the Nonfinance Sub-Index and Finance Sub-Index. It incorporates 10 dimensions, 29 sub-dimensions, and 37 indicators using quantitative and qualitative data collected through the ASM, national census data, business registration data, and credit bureau data with consent (Table 1). The Nonfinance Sub-Index analyzes five dimensions: (i) scale of MSMEs, (ii) employment, (iii) productivity, (iv) market access and innovation, and (v) enabling environment. The Finance Sub-Index analyzes another set of five dimensions: (i) financial depth, (ii) financial stability, (iii) financial infrastructure, (iv) financial technology, and (v) public financial support. Target users of the SME-DI are policymakers responsible for MSME development and financial access in developing Asia. The pilot SME-DI is tested for Southeast Asian countries first, and once improved, may be expanded to other developing Asia subregions.

The SME-DI is a challenging initiative as available MSME data remain limited and firm-level granular data are generally confidential and publicly unavailable. For the first step in designing the SME-DI, this report develops a

---

[1] "East Asia and the Pacific" plus "South Asia," as categorized in this report.
[2] SME-DI covers MSMEs, but uses the term "SME" collectively.

framework design for a feasible SME-DI with a test-run of the pilot index (selected dimensions) for Southeast Asia, and discusses challenges in developing the index. We do not intend to present a complete index at this stage, but raise issues in constructing a more complete index in the future.

Table 1: Conceptual Framework of the SME Development Index

A. Nonfinance Sub-Index

Dimensions (5)	Sub-dimensions (18)	Indicators (20)
1. Scale of MSMEs	1-1 Geographical spread	a. Number of MSMEs by area
	1-2 Industrial structure	b. Number of MSMEs by sector
	1-3 Business generation	c. Length of operations (years)
	1-4 Gender	d. Female owners
2. Employment	2-1 Job creation by SMEs	a. Number of employment by area
	2-2 Industrial structure	b. Number of employment by sector
	2-3 Gender	c. Female employees (% share of total employees)
	2-4 Income	d. Average monthly wage per employee (LCY)
3. Productivity	3-1 Labor productivity	a. Profit (revenue or sales) per employee (LCY)
	3-2 GDP contribution	b. Contribution to GDP [or GVA] (% share of total, by area)
	3-3 Industrial structure	c. Industrial sectors (% share of MSME GDP [or GVA] by sector)
4. Market access and innovation	4-1 Market openness	a. Foreign ownership (domestic or foreign-owned firms)
	4-2 Internationalization	b. MSME exports (LCY amounts)
	4-3 Technology and innovation	c. MSME participation in global value chains
		d. e-commerce (LCY amounts)
		e. Product and process innovation (spend on R&D, LCY)
5. Enabling environment	5-1 Cost of business	a. Operating costs of MSMEs (LCY)
	5-2 Networking and support	b. BDS/incubators (number of beneficiaries)
	5-3 Nonfinance policies	c. National MSME development strategy: coverage of policy actions and implementation
	5-4 Nonfinance regulations	d. Regulations related to MSME sector development

B. Finance Sub-Index

Dimensions (5)	Sub-dimensions (11)	Indicators (17)
1. Financial depth	1-1 Bank credit	a. Access: loans/financing outstanding and market capitalization (LCY)
	1-2 Nonbank finance	b. Products: loan maturity (years), loan interest rate (%), and type of collateral
	1-3 Capital markets	c. Soundness: loan overdue conditions
2. Financial stability	2-1 Finance policies	a. National financial inclusion strategy: coverage of policy actions and implementation
	2-2 Finance regulations	b. Financial sector development strategy: coverage of policy actions and implementation
		c. Regulations related to MSME access to finance
3. Financial infrastructure	3-1 Credit bureau system	a. Company data availed in credit bureau (number)
	3-2 Secured lending system	b. Coverage of pledged assets in collateral registry
		c. Usage of credit bureau data and collateral registry
4. Financial technology	4-1 Digital financial services	a. Digital payments (LCY amounts)
		b. Mobile credit and savings (LCY amounts)
		c. E-money accounts opened (number)
		d. DFS solution providers (number)
5. Public financial support	5-1 Soft loans	a. Subsidized loans outstanding to MSMEs (LCY)
	5-2 Public credit guarantees	b. Guaranteed loans outstanding to MSMEs (LCY)
	5-3 Other finance measures	c. Recovery amounts of credit guarantees (LCY)
		d. MSMEs accepted for subsidized loans and public credit guarantees (number)

BDS = business development service; DFS = digital financial service; GDP = gross domestic product; GVA = gross value added; LCY = local currency; MSME = micro, small, and medium-sized enterprise; R&D = research and development.
Source: Authors' compilation.

MSME Landscape in Southeast Asia

This section reviews the landscape for MSME development and access to finance in Southeast Asia, given the design of the pilot SME-DI. MSMEs have driven much of the economic growth in Southeast Asia over the past 10 years (Table 2). Based on national classifications, during 2010–2019, MSMEs in the region accounted for 97.2% of all enterprises, 69.4% of the national workforce, and 41.1% of a country's gross domestic product (GDP) (ADB, 2020a). MSMEs dominate the business environment in the region. The share of MSMEs to total enterprises showed almost no change over the decade (a negligible compound annual decline of 0.3%). The share of MSME employees to total employees grew slightly (a compound annual growth of 0.8%) and MSME contributions to GDP expanded moderately (a compound annual growth of 2.3%). These facts demonstrate the dynamics of MSMEs driving national economies in the region. Further strengthening their dynamism will boost national productivity.

In general, most MSMEs operate within small domestic markets in relatively stable businesses—such as distributive trade—alongside a small base of growth-oriented MSMEs or entrepreneurs with innovative, global visions. Only a small number of MSMEs have been exposed or have access to global markets. However, in some countries, MSMEs are influencing international trade. In Indonesia, Malaysia, and Thailand (the only countries reporting), they contributed an average 20.4% of export value during 2010–2018 (a negligible compound annual contraction of 0.05%). Overall, MSME participation in global value chains is limited. Their access to global markets remains a major challenge. Enhancing MSME internationalization will contribute to increased national productivity, but the ongoing coronavirus disease (COVID-19) and associated quarantine measures created new business risks to globalized MSMEs due to supply chain disruptions and compressed demand for their products and services (ADB, 2020b).

Poor access to finance has been one of the most critical factors inhibiting the growth of MSMEs. In Southeast Asia, bank lending to MSMEs made up 14.8% of a country's GDP and 16.9% of total bank lending on average during 2010–2019 (ADB, 2020a). The MSME credit market is small with sluggish growth. The share of MSME loans to national GDP and total bank loans has been gradually decreasing (a compound annual decline of 1.3% and 0.3%, respectively). MSMEs' nonperforming loans (NPLs) as a percentage of total MSME bank loans were an average 4.1% during the same period, a 2.5% decrease at a compound annual rate, but higher than the overall bank average (2.0%). Given the region's bank-centered financial system, limited access to bank credit constrains MSME business operations and expansion plans. Stakeholders of MSME development identify limited access to bank credit as a key constraint and primary reason why MSME productivity is low nationally.

Governments in the region see MSME development as a policy priority for accelerating economic diversification and enhancing inclusive growth. Most Southeast Asian countries have a long-term policy framework on MSME development in line with their national development plans and goals. As part of this, central banks and financial authorities promote financial inclusion, including enhanced MSME access to formal financial services.

Table 2: MSMEs in Southeast Asia

Country	Number of MSMEs (% of total)	Employment by MSMEs (% of total)	MSME contribution to GDP (%)	MSME export values (% of total)	MSME bank loans to GDP (%)	MSME bank loans to total bank loans (%)	MSME NPLs to MSME bank loans (%)
Brunei Darussalam	97.2	57.3	35.5	–	0.1	0.2	–
Cambodia	99.8	71.8	–	–	–	–	–
Indonesia	99.99	97.0	61.1	14.4	7.0	19.6	3.6
Lao PDR	99.8	82.4	–	–	8.5	19.8	–
Malaysia	98.5	66.2	38.3	17.3	18.5	14.6	3.7
Myanmar	89.9	–	–	–	1.0	4.8	–
Philippines	99.5	63.2	35.7	–	3.2	6.1	5.8
Singapore	99.5	71.4	44.7	–	15.1	5.8	4.2
Thailand	99.8	85.5	43.0	28.7	30.3	30.9	4.7
Viet Nam	97.2	38.0	–	–	–	–	–

GDP = gross domestic product; Lao PDR = Lao People's Democratic Republic; MSME = micro, small, and medium-sized enterprise; NPL = nonperforming loan.
Note: The latest available data in 2014–2019, except MSME contribution to GDP in the Philippines (2006).
Source: ADB Asia SME Monitor 2020 database.

Exploration of Index

1.   Global MSME Data Initiatives

There are several stages to developing an index that measures specific aspects of MSMEs and policy interventions in Asia. This section compares existing regional and global MSME data initiatives and MSME indexes. It reviews the type of study performed, geographic area covered, frequency of data updates, specific MSME data collected, and methodology. Studies can be thematic, country-level data analysis, or other data analysis. The geographic area includes the overall number of countries and the number of Asia and Pacific nations. The frequency of data updates is usually annual, but can be ad hoc or another time period. Specific MSME data involves capital market data, lending data, overall landscape for MSMEs, and MSME policies, among others. Various kinds of methods such as surveys, interviews, and partnerships for sharing data comprise the methodology. We examine existing MSME knowledge products covering the Asia and Pacific region: (i) ADB's ASM; (ii) Organisation for Economic Co-operation and Development (OECD) SME and Entrepreneurship Outlook; (iii) Financing SMEs and Entrepreneurs: An OECD Scoreboard, a.k.a. "OECD Scoreboard"; (iv) OECD and the Economic Research Institute for ASEAN and East Asia (ERIA) Association of Southeast Asian Nations (ASEAN) SME Policy Index; (v) Credibility Index for SMEs developed by the Asia Professional Education Network (APEN) with the Advanced Institute of Industrial Technology (AIIT), Japan; (vi) International Trade Centre (ITC) SME Competitiveness Index; (vii) International Finance Corporation (IFC) MSME Finance Gap; (viii) World Bank Enterprise Surveys; and (ix) World Bank Doing Business Indicators (Table 3).

ADB's Asia Small and Medium-Sized Enterprise Monitor

The Asia Small and Medium-Sized Enterprise Monitor (ASM) is a knowledge-sharing product developed by ADB as a key resource for MSME development policies in Asia and the Pacific. Produced annually, the ASM reviews financial and nonfinancial conditions of MSMEs nationally and regionally. The inaugural volume (ASM 2013) was published in 2014 with 14 countries from five ADB regions (Central Asia, East Asia, South Asia, Southeast Asia, and the Pacific). The country coverage was extended to 20 countries in the ASM 2014, published in 2015.[3] While ASM 2013 and 2014 focused specifically on MSME access to finance, ASM 2020 extends its analytical coverage to nonfinancial issues affecting MSME development.

Its country and regional review (Volume I) offers cross-country analyses on financial and nonfinancial issues for MSME development. It has three review dimensions with 14 sub-dimensions for analysis: (i) MSME development (scale of MSMEs, employment, business productivity, market access, technology and innovation, and networking and support); (ii) access to finance (bank credit, public financing and guarantees, nonbank financing, digital financial services, capital markets, and financial infrastructure); and (iii) policies and regulations (MSME development and

---

[3]   (i) Kazakhstan, the Kyrgyz Republic, and Tajikistan in Central Asia; (ii) the People's Republic of China (PRC), Republic of Korea, and Mongolia in East Asia; (iii) Bangladesh, India, and Sri Lanka in South Asia; (iv) Cambodia, Indonesia, the Lao People's Democratic Republic (Lao PDR), Malaysia, Myanmar, the Philippines, Thailand, and Viet Nam in Southeast Asia; and (v) Fiji, Papua New Guinea, and Solomon Islands in the Pacific.

financial inclusion). It analyzes these dimensions using data collected from partner institutions of ADB developing members using a standardized ASM data request form.

OECD SME and Entrepreneurship Outlook

The OECD SME and Entrepreneurship Outlook was launched in 2002 as the OECD Small and Medium Enterprise Outlook, assuming its current format and title in 2005. The most recent version was published in 2019; it contains 6 dimensions and 29 sub-dimensions. The six dimensions are (i) Institutional and Regulatory Framework, (ii) Market Conditions, (iii) Infrastructure, (iv) Access to Finance, (v) Access to Skills, and (vi) Access to Innovation Assets. The Outlook 2019 analyzes data for 2014–2017 for the 34 countries that were OECD members as of 2014. In addition to the quantitative analysis of the six dimensions, Outlook 2019 also furnishes descriptive statistics for the 36 member countries as of its publication date in a separate Country Profile section. The Asia and Pacific countries within the OECD include Australia, Japan, New Zealand, and the Republic of Korea.

As noted, there are 29 separate variables (sub-dimensions) that form the six dimensions, with 4-6 variables per dimension. The Institutional and Regulatory Framework includes regulation, courts and laws, land and housing, public governance, competition, and taxation. Market Conditions encompass the domestic market, global markets, public procurement, and trade and investment. Infrastructure comprises logistics, energy, research and development (R&D) and innovation, and internet and information and communications technology (ICT). Access to Finance includes self-funding, debt, the financial system, and alternative instruments. Access to Skills uses adult literacy, labor market, entrepreneurial culture, training, and education. Access to Innovation Assets contains technology, R&D, organization and processes, marketing, and data.

OECD Scoreboard

The OECD Scoreboard is a publication produced annually since 2012. The 2012 edition contained 13 core indicators for financing SMEs and entrepreneurs from 18 countries covering 2007–2010; the 2020 version has 17 indicators for 48 countries for 2017–2018. According to the OECD, these indicators meet the following criteria: usefulness, data availability, feasibility, timeliness, and comparability.[4] The OECD constructs the indicators mainly from supply-side data; standardized forms are used to gather data from banks, other financial institutions, and government agencies.

There are 22 separate variables comprising the 17 indicators, including total lending (overall and SME), new lending (overall and SME), short- versus long-term SME loans, direct government SME loans, government loan guarantees, interest rates (overall and SME), collateral (SME), and bankruptcies (SME), among others. In short, the OECD Scoreboard contains lending/banking sector data, nonbank sector data, and capital market data.

Among the 48 countries in the 2020 edition, 11 are from the Asia and Pacific region:[5] Australia, Indonesia, Israel, Japan, Kazakhstan, Malaysia, New Zealand, the PRC, the Republic of Korea, Thailand, and Turkey (including 5 ADB developing member countries). There are 29 European countries, 4 from South America, 3 from North America, and 1 from Africa. For each, there is a country snapshot with an analysis of the panel data/scoreboard, for example, 2007–2018 for the 18 original countries.

---

[4] OECD iLibrary. Annex A. Methodology for producing the national scoreboards. https://www.oecd-ilibrary.org/sites/061fe03d-en/1/4/1/index.html?itemId=/content/publication/061fe03d-en&_csp_=5d0be09b32d3f3a6aa507a1c266f5551&itemIGO=oecd&itemContentType=book.

[5] The OECD Scoreboard considers Israel and Turkey as Asia and Pacific countries.

ASEAN SME Policy Index

In 2014 and 2018, the OECD and ERIA launched the ASEAN SME Policy Index to present the policy landscape for SME development across ASEAN countries by building on the OECD methodology (ERIA and OECD, 2014). This index assesses the scope and intensity of SME development policies across eight dimensions: (i) productivity, technology and innovation, (ii) environmental policies targeting SMEs, (iii) access to finance, (iv) access to market and internationalization, (v) institutional framework, (vi) legislation, regulation and tax, (vii) entrepreneurial education and skills, and (viii) social enterprises and inclusive entrepreneurship. These 8 dimensions comprise 25 sub-dimensions, which are measured using three scales: (i) planning and design stage, (ii) implementation stage, and (iii) monitoring and evaluation stage.

Nearly 50 stakeholders assess SME development policies on two parallel fronts. Government ministries evaluate their own SME policies and share relevant data with the OECD and ERIA, while they conduct independent studies to collect and analyze data from key stakeholders and private sector representatives. Respondents score the strengths and weaknesses of the present SME policies on a scale from 1 to 6, with higher scores indicating a better level of policy development and implementation for each sub-dimension. The cross-sectional data are analyzed to compare participating ASEAN countries and develop an ASEAN benchmark after standardizing all eight dimensions on the 1–6 scale.[6]

Credibility Index for SMEs

In 2017, APEN, in cooperation with the AIIT, developed the Credibility Index for SMEs (CIS), which is a tool to evaluate the operational credibility of SMEs and to enhance SME competitiveness in ASEAN (APEN and AIIT, 2017). The index applies to both established SMEs (more than 5 years of operations) and emerging SMEs. The CIS for established SMEs assesses how well ASEAN SMEs operate with a set of questions. They comprise 6 dimensions, covering 25 sub-dimensions: (i) management strength, (ii) technical capabilities, (iii) sales capabilities, (iv) human resource capabilities, (v) organization strength, and (vi) financial strength. The CIS for emerging SMEs is similar, yet more concise, than the version for established SMEs. Participating ASEAN universities subsequently adapted the CIS to local conditions and translated it into local languages. The participating countries include Brunei Darussalam, Cambodia, Indonesia, the Lao People's Democratic Republic (Lao PDR), Malaysia, and the Philippines.

Under the APEN project, qualitative data obtained from national field surveys were cross-sectional in the form of a "Yes" or "No" answer or scores between 1 and 5 posed to SME owners or managers. For example, in the "Management Strength" dimension, one question is "Do you have any proper facilities for the processing of emission, waste, recycling, etc.?". Participating universities scored all the six dimensions and plotting the results on radar charts.[7]

SME Competitiveness Outlook

The ITC publishes its annual SME Competitiveness Outlook to assess SME development and financing needed in 85 countries worldwide to facilitate implementation of the United Nations Sustainable Development Goals 8 and 9. This report provides an SME Competitiveness Index with 3 dimensions, covering 39 sub-dimensions: (i) firm capabilities, (ii) business ecosystem, and (iii) national environment. The first dimension relates to SME's ability to manage resources under its control. The second covers resources and competencies necessary for enhancing a firm's competitiveness. The third captures government functionality and policy implementation. Each dimension

6   OECD/ERIA. 2018. SME Policy Index: ASEAN 2018: Boosting Competitiveness and Inclusive Growth. Paris: OECD Publishing/Jakarta: ERIA. https://asean.org/wp-content/uploads/2018/08/Report-ASEAN-SME-Policy-Index-2018.pdf.
7   Asia Professional Education Network (APEN). 2017. APEN JAIF Project Final Report. 31 August. http://www.apen.asia/?page_id=1763.

is assessed with three aspects, (i) capacity to compete (enterprise efficiency), (ii) capacity to connect (information and knowledge gathering/exploitation), and (iii) capacity to change (human and financial capital investments).[8]

The panel analysis uses time series data from 2006–2018 from various secondary sources—such as the World Bank's Enterprise Surveys, Ease of Doing Business Index and Logistics Performance Index, the International Monetary Fund's (IMF) World Economic Outlook, and ITC's Market Access Map. The empirics examined the reference level, strengths, and weaknesses in competitiveness among small, medium-sized, and large enterprises based on the work of Papke and Woolridge (2008). The World Bank Enterprise Surveys are the source for firm size categories and the 0–100 scale used in the analysis. The strengths and weaknesses are relative to a reference level based on per capita GDP. All 39 sub-dimensions are translated into this 0–100 scale.

IFC MSME Finance Gap Report

The IFC first published its MSME Finance Gap in 2010 in conjunction with McKinsey & Co., and updated it in 2013 and 2017 in partnership with the World Bank Group. This more recent collaboration resulted in a change in methodology from the original publication that allowed cross-country comparisons.[9] In short, the methodology first estimates the potential demand for financing in emerging economies and compares it with current supply. The difference between the two is the "finance gap." Rajan and Zingales (1998) offer the operating assumptions about the dependence of a given industry on external finance, which is the starting point for the MSME Finance Gap.

Benchmarking is the first empirical step. The financing needs of MSMEs in 10 advanced economies form the baseline; these economies are chosen both because they are high-income and because they rank highest on the "Getting Credit" module of the World Bank Doing Business Index. MSME categories include industry (manufacturing, services, or retail); size; and age. The World Bank Enterprise Surveys furnish the data necessary, in conjunction with benchmarking, for estimating the potential demand for MSME finance in the second step. Both the IMF Financial Access Surveys and the OECD SME Scoreboard provide the current supply of MSME finance in the third step.

The 2017 MSME Finance Gap covers 128 countries, of which 112 are low- and middle-income countries. Of the 128 nations, 29 are ADB developing member countries. Updates are ad hoc, with data collection focusing on general indicators for the MSME landscape, lending and banking data, and nonbank data.

World Bank Enterprise Surveys

The World Bank Enterprise Surveys began in 2002. They are global in coverage and consist of country-level data using a standardized SME definition.[10] Each year, a different group of countries is updated, so that an individual country might be covered every 3-6 years. For example, Viet Nam was first included in the Enterprise Surveys in 2005, then again in 2009, and most recently in 2015. The data are available by country and by year or as a panel for a given country. As of October 2020, there are data for 36 Asia and Pacific countries for various years.

For each country, the Enterprise Surveys collects firm-level data on a wide variety of topics using slightly different surveys based on industry (Manufacturing versus Services). The Enterprise Surveys uses random sampling to ensure surveyed firms are representative of the overall population according to size, location, industry, among

---

[8]   International Trade Centre. *SME Competitiveness Outlook 2019: Big Money for Small Business – Financing the Sustainable Development Goals.* https://www.intracen.org/publication/smeco2019.

[9]   IFC. 2017. *MSME FINANCE GAP: Assessment of the Shortfalls and Opportunities in Financing Micro, Small and Medium Enterprises in Emerging Markets.* Washington, DC. https://www.smefinanceforum.org/sites/default/files/Data%20Sites%20downloads/MSME%20Report.pdf.

[10]   The Enterprise Surveys defines small firms as having 5-19 employees, medium firms as having 20-99, and large firms employing 100 or more employees. https://www.enterprisesurveys.org/en/methodology.

others. As such, the surveys are not targeted specifically at SMEs. But the data allow cross-country comparisons of SMEs given that SMEs are generally the vast majority of firms. Topics include general information; infrastructure and services provided to the firm; sales and supplies; degree of competition; innovation; capacity; land and permits; crime; finance; business–government relations; labor (number of employees, among others); business environment; and the firm's performance.

World Bank Doing Business Report

The World Bank offers another product, the Doing Business Report, which was updated annually for 17 years until 2020. The first report appeared in autumn 2003 for the year 2004, featuring thematic data across more than 130 countries covering five dimensions: Starting a Business, Hiring and Firing Workers, Enforcing a Contract, Getting Credit, and Closing a Business. The most recent Doing Business Report was published in October 2019 for the year 2020 and encompasses 190 countries involving 12 dimensions: Starting a Business, Dealing with Construction Permits, Getting Electricity, Registering Property, Getting Credit, Protecting Minority Investors, Paying Taxes, Trading across Borders, Enforcing Contracts, Resolving Insolvency, Employing Workers, and Contracting with the Government. The latter two dimensions are not considered when constructing the Doing Business 2020 Ease of Doing Business Index/Ranking.

Theoretically, the 12 dimensions capture five separate aspects of running a business: opening, getting a location, accessing finance, dealing with day-to-day operations, and operating in a secure business environment. According to the Doing Business 2020 Report, these dimensions were selected based on "background papers developing the methodology for most of the Doing Business indicator sets have established the importance of rules and regulations that Doing Business measures for economic outcomes such as trade volumes, foreign direct investment, market capitalization in stock exchanges, and private credit as a percentage of GDP" (Doing Business 2020, p.18).

Value-Addition of ADB SME Development Index

The comparison of existing MSME indexes mentioned above and the ADB SME-DI shows similarities in terms of index dimensions and differences in terms of methodology, such as data collection and analysis. For example, both CIS and SME-DI cover similar policy dimensions, such as financial inclusion, profit, market openness, and internationalization. On the other hand, the difference is that the CIS relies upon the self-assessment of SME owners or managers, whereas the SME-DI calculates aggregate and firm-level data with actual values provided by the governments and private sector stakeholders through ASM and with consent to use the firm-level data.

The ASEAN SME Policy Index of the OECD and ERIA also have similarities with the SME-DI in terms of dimensions, but not in methodology. For example, the "financial depth," "financial stability," and "financial infrastructure" dimensions of the SME-DI are similar to the "access to finance" dimension of the SME Policy Index as shown in Table 3. The "market access and innovation" dimension of the SME-DI is similar to the "access to market and internationalization" dimension of the SME Policy Index. On the other hand, data for the ASEAN SME Policy Index are entirely cross-sectional, designed to construct panel data over time, with scoring and weighting qualitative, while the SME-DI uses a more quantitative approach for both cross-sectional and panel data.

Table 3: Global MSME Data Initiatives in Asia and the Pacific

Item	Asia Small and Medium-Sized Enterprise Monitor (ASM)	SME and Entrepreneurship Outlook	Financing SMEs and Entrepreneurs (OECD Scoreboard)	ASEAN SME Policy Index	Credibility Index for SMEs	SME Competitiveness Outlook	SME Development Index (Concept)
Lead organization	ADB	OECD	OECD	OECD and ERIA	APEN and AIIT	ITC	ADB
Year launched	2014 (ASM 2013)	2002	2012	2014	2017	2015	–
Latest edition	2020	2019	2020	2018	2017	2019	–
Dimension	3	6	5	8	6	3	10
1	MSME development	Institutional and regulatory framework	Allocation and structure of bank credit to SMEs	Productivity, technology, and innovation	Management strength	Firm capabilities	Scale of MSMEs
2	Access to finance	Market conditions	Extent of public support for SME finance	Environmental policies targeting SMEs	Technical capabilities	Business ecosystem	Employment
3	Policies and regulations	Infrastructure	Credit costs and conditions	Access to finance	Sales capabilities	National environment	Productivity
4		Access to finance	Nonbank sources of finance	Access to market and internationalization	Human resource capabilities		Market access and innovation
5		Access to skills	Financial health	Institutional framework	Organization strength		Enabling environment
6		Access to innovation assets		Legislation, regulation, and tax	Financial strength		Financial depth
7				Entrepreneurial education and skills			Financial stability
8				Social enterprises and inclusive entrepreneurship			Financial infrastructure
9							Financial technology
10							Public financial support
Sub-dimension	14	29	25	25	25	39	29
Data	Cross-sectional and time series	Cross-sectional	Cross-sectional (intent to create a time series)	Cross-sectional (intent to create a time series)	Cross-sectional	Cross-sectional and time series	Cross-sectional and time series
Methodology	Quantitative and qualitative national surveys	Median comparison	Descriptive national surveys	Qualitative national surveys	Qualitative national surveys	Median comparison	Two-stage PCA (with qualitative assessments)
Participating countries	10 ASEAN member states (ASM 2020). Country coverage to be expanded to other Asian subregions.	OECD member countries (including Australia, Japan, New Zealand, and the Republic of Korea)	48 countries (2020 edition) (including Australia, Indonesia, Israel, Japan, Kazakhstan, Malaysia, New Zealand, the People's Republic of China, the Republic of Korea, Thailand, and Turkey)	10 ASEAN member states	6 ASEAN member states (Brunei Darussalam, Cambodia, Indonesia, the Lao People's Democratic Republic (Lao PDR), Malaysia, and the Philippines)	85 countries (2020 edition) (including Armenia, Azerbaijan, Bangladesh, Bhutan, Cambodia, Georgia, Indonesia, Kazakhstan, the Kyrgyz Republic, the Lao PDR, Mongolia, Myanmar, Nepal, Pakistan, the Philippines, the Russian Federation, Tajikistan, Timor-Leste, Turkey, and Viet Nam)	10 ASEAN member states (for pilot index). Country coverage to be expanded to other Asian subregions.
Remarks	Country and regional reviews	SME performance and the degree of entrepreneurship	Finance and entrepreneurship scoreboard	Policy landscape relates to SME development and policy implementation	SMEs' competitiveness	SME competitiveness at the macro level	Finance and nonfinance indices

ADB = Asian Development Bank; AIIT = Advanced Institute of Industrial Technology; APEN = Asia Professional Education Network; ASEAN = Association of Southeast Asian Nations; ERIA = Economic Research Institute for ASEAN and East Asia; ITC = International Trade Centre; MSME = micro, small, and medium-sized enterprise; OECD = Organisation for Economic Co-operation and Development; PCA = principal component analysis; SME = small and medium-sized enterprise.
Sources: APEN and AIIT (2017), ITC (2019), OECD (2019a and 2019b), OECD and ERIA (2018). Recomposed.

2.   Review of Index Development

The SME-DI builds upon several composite indexes published over the past decade that capture various economic outcomes in Asia and the Pacific and the world (Table 4). As the previous section mainly addressed the qualitative scoring models of SME indexes, this section reviews literature on the development of policy indexes that use a multivariate analytical approach.

The seminal work of Adelman and Morris (1973) quantifies the socioeconomic development of 74 countries by using factor analysis with 41 social, political, and economic indicators covering the 1950s and early 1960s.

Bo and Woo (2008) measures the level of economic integration in the Asia and Pacific region. The authors cover 17 economies over 1990–2005. Using a two-stage principal component analysis (PCA), they find that Singapore and Hong Kong, China are the most integrated in the Asia and Pacific region, while Indonesia and the PRC are the least integrated (Bo and Woo, 2008). The SME-DI seeks to measure the best conditions for SME development in a manner analogous to Bo and Woo's (2008) concept of most economically integrated.

Debuque-Gonzalez and Gochoco-Bautista (2013) offer financial conditions indexes (FCIs) for five Asian economies: Hong Kong, China; Japan; Malaysia; the PRC; and the Republic of Korea. The purpose of the FCI is to highlight areas of financial stress in a given economy. The authors apply PCA to quarterly data over varying time frames to construct their FCIs; for example, Japan has data from Q4 1980 to Q3 2011 whereas Singapore has data from Q1 1983 to Q1 2011. The authors then compile a new FCI for Asia based on the averages for the five economies. This is also an SME-DI objective: to move from individual economies such as Cambodia to subregional indexes such as Cambodia, the Lao PDR, Myanmar, and Viet Nam, and then to ASEAN as a whole.

The World Bank publishes its Logistics Performance Index (LPI) biennially as part of its "Connecting to Compete" report, with the first in 2007 and the most recent in 2018. The LPI also features PCA as its empirical method, using six dimensions and six indicators to assess the quality and reliability of national supply chains in 167 economies (World Bank, 2018). The LPI lends itself readily to policy prescriptions for improving logistics; the SME-DI has a similar goal for policymaking with regard to SME development.

Gygli, Haelg, and Sturm (2018) constructed a composite index called the KOF Globalization Index covering 209 countries for 1970–2015. This index influenced the SME-DI in several notable ways, one in fact and two that are aspirational. The former is that the KOF features more sophisticated empirical methods than most indexes. While the KOF utilizes PCA, Park and Claveria (2018) describe it as "multi-stage." As described in the subsequent Analytical Approach section, the SME-DI also goes beyond the typical PCA. In terms of aspiration, the KOF is the most widely used globalization index in the literature (Gygli, Haelg, and Sturm, 2018, citing Potrafke, 2015). The second is that the KOF has unusual flexibility in measuring both de jure globalization and de facto globalization, thereby differentiating between what is stated in policy versus what occurs in practice. We expect the SME-DI will become the standard for capturing SME development and that it will display this kind of flexibility as it evolves.

Park and Claveria (2018) built the Asia-Pacific Regional Cooperation and Integration Index covering 158 countries for 2006–2016. Their work advances on Bo and Woo (2008) in several important ways. Whereas the former studies only 17 countries in the Asia and Pacific region, the latter is global, covering nearly 160 nations. The former has 4 dimensions and 8 indicators to measure economic integration, while the latter is broader and deeper with 6 dimensions and 26 indicators, with an additional emphasis on cooperation. Most importantly, while both sets of authors use two-stage PCA on their respective panel datasets, Park and Claveria (2018) derive more benefit from their panel in terms of normalizing and imputing data. Similarly, we see the use of panel data as essential for making the SME-DI a robust tool, both now and in the future, and view it as a clear contribution beyond current SME indexes that only employ cross-sectional analysis.

Huh and Park (2017) demonstrate a systematic process for applying two-stage principal component analysis to construct an index. We defer discussion of their work to Section 4.

Table 4: Theoretical Foundation of the SME Development Index

Article	Construct/Idea	Application to SME-DI
Bo and Woo (2008)	Specific economic outcome: integration	Specific outcome: SME development
Debuque-Gonzalez and Gochoco-Bautista (2013)	Scaling from national to regional index	Individual ASEAN countries to CLMV index to ASEAN index
World Bank (2018)	Ready tool for policymakers to improve logistics	Ready tool for policymakers to improve SME development
Gygli, Haelg, and Sturm (2018)	KOF globalization index uses more advanced empirics. KOF globalization index is the most widely used. KOF globalization index has separate measures for de jure and de facto globalization.	SME-DI uses dynamic factor modeling and OLS in addition to the usual PCA. SME-DI aspires to be the most widely used index for SME development. SME-DI aspires toward operational flexibility.
Park and Claveria (2018)	Maximizing the benefit from panel data	SME-DI analyzes panel data over the typical cross-sectional approach.
Huh and Park (2017)	Utilizing two-stage PCA to construct Index.	two-stage PCA is the primary method behind the SME-DI (see Section 4)

ASEAN = Association of Southeast Asian Nations; CLMV = Cambodia, Lao People's Democratic Republic, Myanmar, and Viet Nam; KOF = Konjunkturforschungsstelle (Swiss economic institute); OLS = ordinary least squares; PCA = principal component analysis; SME = small and medium-sized enterprise; SME-DI = Small and Medium-Sized Enterprise Development Index.
Source: Authors' compilation.

Methodology

1.　Analytical Approach

In the first step, we review the aggregate MSME data captured by ASM 2020 and the granular enterprise data that we received exclusively from select Southeast Asian countries for the test-run of the empirical analysis. We use PCA to estimate weights of selected variables and normalize different indicators to create a composite index in the condition of sufficient sample size. However, in case of limited sample size, dynamic factor modeling (DFM) will be considered. In this model, we use cross-section analysis with time series to increase the sample size. Another approach, principal component pursuit (PCP) or robust PCA, will be also considered, given the possible impact of outliers. PCP can recover low-rank and sparse components. After the review of available data, we will decide on a single method for the initial quantitative analysis (PCA, DFM, or PCP) (Box 1). We interpret the result of PCA, DFM, or PCP as higher weight of the sub-dimension indicating higher impact on the dimension. In the second step, as needed, we may use ordinary least squares (OLS) for supplementary analysis to explain the results of the initial analysis. This may be combined with a qualitative scoring method using a specially elaborated assessment matrix as necessary.

Two-Stage Principal Component Analysis

Among possible analytical options, this section develops two-stage PCA for the SME-DI. PCA is a statistical technique that, "partitions the variance in a set of variables and uses it to determine weights that maximize the resulting principal component's variation. In effect, the derived principal component is the variable that captures variations in data to the maximum extent possible" (Huh and Park, 2017). PCA is a familiar method for constructing indexes (Huh and Park, 2017; Park and Claveria, 2018), so we forego further explanation of the initial estimation to focus on what is known as "two-stage PCA" (Huh and Park, 2017). Here, PCA is first employed to find the relevant principal components for each dimension, and then, in the second stage, PCA is used again to estimate the composite index from the components.

Given a sufficient sample size of enterprise data, we use two-stage PCA to create the composite index or SME-DI, referring to Bo and Woo (2008), Huh and Park (2017), and Park and Claveria (2018). If panel data are available, we assume X_{txp} as multidimensional data for obtaining the weights for estimating the SME-DI, where t is total number of periods and p is the number of dimensions. Given that R_{pxp} is the correlation matrix of indicators under the p dimension, the principal component Z_i^t is defined as

$$Z_i^t = X\alpha^{it} \qquad \lambda_{it} = \text{var}\,(X\alpha^{it}) \tag{1}$$

where λ_i ($i = 1, ..., p$) is defined as the ith eigenvalue and α^i as the corresponding i^{th} eigenvector of the correlation matrix R_{pxp}, with the normalization condition of $\alpha^{i\prime}\,\alpha^i = 1$. The ith eigenvalue is equal to the variance of the ith principal component. The first principal component is created as the linear combination of the indicators with the largest variance, followed by the second, third, and the pth principal component as another linear combination of the indicators orthogonal to all the other principal components until the smallest variance.

Based on the first-stage PCA mentioned above, the composite index (the final weight) or SME-DI is estimated by

$$\text{SME-DI} = \frac{\sum_{i=1}^{p} X\alpha^i \lambda^i}{\sum_{i=1}^{p} \lambda_i} \tag{2}$$

Box 1: Analytical Options for the SME Development Index

Two-stage principal component analysis (PCA)

$$Z_i^t = X\alpha^{it} \qquad \lambda_{it} = \text{var}\,(X\alpha^{it}) \tag{1}$$

$$\text{SME-DI} = \frac{\sum_{i=1}^{p} X\alpha^i \lambda^i}{\sum_{i=1}^{p} \lambda_i} \tag{2}$$

λ_i (i = 1, ..., p) = eigenvalue α^i = eigenvector
X_{txp} (t = total number of periods, p = number of dimensions)

Dynamic factor modeling (DFM)

Dynamic factor modeling (DFM) is a type of estimation technique that "manages to combine, from a descriptive point of view (not probabilistic), the cross-section analysis through principal component analysis (PCA) and the time series dimension of data through a linear regression model" (Federici and Mazzitelli, 2005). These authors also describe DFM as "a statistical multiway analysis technique, where quantitative 'units * variables * times' are considered." DFM is an appropriate technique when the sample size is limited.

Stock and Watson (2010) note that, "the premise of a dynamic factor model is that a few latent dynamic factors, f_t, drive the co-movements of a high-dimensional vector of time-series variables, X_t, which is also affected by a vector of mean-zero idiosyncratic disturbances, e_t. These idiosyncratic disturbances arise from measurement error and from special features that are specific to an individual series. The latent factors follow a time series process, which is commonly taken to be a vector autoregression (VAR). In equations, the dynamic factor model is

$$X_t = \lambda\,(L)f_t + e_t \tag{3}$$

$$f_t = \Psi(L)_{ft-1} + \eta \tag{4}$$

where there are N series, X_t and e_t are N×1; there are q dynamic factors, f_t and η_t are q×1, L is the lag operator, and the lag polynomial matrices $\lambda\,(L)$ and $\Psi(L)$ are N×q and q×q, respectively" (Stock and Watson, 2010).

In plain language, DFM is a two-stage factor analysis. In the first stage, the analysis resembles PCA, where there is the discovery of the factors that primarily account for the item/phenomenon being measured. In the second stage, these factors are being analyzed over time. Recall the equation for PCA:

$$\frac{\sum_{i=1}^{p} X\alpha^i \lambda^i}{\sum_{i=1}^{p} \lambda_i} = S_T \tag{2}$$

This equation is a variance–covariance matrix representing the variability due to the difference between the overall average of the units and each single unit. It is "within times," meaning cross-sectional. Let us call this matrix S_T (Federici and Mazzitelli, 2005).

continued on next page

Box 1 continued

To this must be added another matrix accounting for the difference "between times," or time series. Let us call this matrix S_T^*. This matrix is modeled via linear regression of the overall average variable X for each single variable j at time t (Frederici and Mazzitelli, 2005):

$$X_{jt} = a_j + b_j t + e = S_T^*$$
(5)

The new Small and Medium-Sized Enterprise Development Index (SME-DI), as estimated via DFM, is the sum of the two matrices:

$$SME\text{-}DI = S_T + S_T^*$$
(6)

Principal component pursuit (PCP)

If the data not only represent a limited sample size, but also contain an outlier, we then resort to principal component pursuit (PCP). Several researchers have described PCP as a robust form of PCA (Candes, Li, Ma, and Wright, 2009; Bouwmans and Zahzah, 2014; Shaukat, Rao, and Khan, 2016). According to Candes et al. (2009), when data points are stacked as column vectors of a matrix M such that

$$M = L_0 + N_0$$
(7)

where L_0 has low-rank and N_0 is a small perturbation matrix, given a large data matrix M. The classical PCA seeks the best rank k estimate of L_0 by solving (ibid, p.2)

$$\text{minimize } ||M - L||, \text{ subject to rank}(L) \le k$$
(8)

As the authors note, however, a single outlier (or, in their words, "grossly corrupted entry") in matrix M "could render the estimated L arbitrarily far from the true L_0" (p.2). What is needed is a method "to recover a low-rank matrix L_0 from highly corrupted measurements $M = L_0 + S_0$. Unlike the small noise term N_0 in classical PCA, the entries in S_0 can have arbitrarily large magnitude, and their support is assumed to *sparse* (their italics) but unknown" (p.2).

Based upon their research, Candes, et al. (2009) stipulate that the PCP estimate solving

$$\text{minimize } || L ||^* + \ell || S ||_1, \text{ subject to } L + S = M$$
(9)

"exactly recovers the low-rank L_0 and the sparse S_0."

Ordinary least squares (OLS)

As a supplementary analysis to the PCA, DFM, and PCP, we may also use ordinary least squares (OLS). Prior academic work recommends OLS as an additional method for index construction (c.f. Abeyasekera, 2005). We expect that linear regression will add more nuance to our main analyses, particularly with regard to SME performance. We will estimate the following:

$$SME\ Performance_{i,t} = \gamma X_{i,t} + \delta Y_{j,t} + \eta Z_{j,t} + C + \varepsilon$$
(10)

where $X_{i,t}$ is a vector of observable firm-specific factors (for example, number of employees, industrial sector), and γ is a vector of coefficients; $Y_{j,t}$ is a vector of observable financial factors (for example, bank credit, nonbank financing), and δ is a vector of coefficients; $Z_{j,t}$ is a vector of observable nonfinancial factors (for example, business productivity, market access) and η is a vector of coefficients, C is the constant or intercept, and ε is the error term.

2.   Data Selection

For the test-run of the two-stage PCA, we prepare two sets of data: (i) aggregate MSME data captured by the ASM 2020 with time series and (ii) granular company data in Cambodia that Credit Bureau Cambodia allowed us to use for the purpose of designing the SME-DI. It should be noted that, at this stage, indicators we expect under the conceptual framework of the SME-DI (Table 1) are not fully available nationally. More work is needed to capture expected indicators through data-sharing agreements with statistics offices, business registration offices, credit bureaus, government authorities (SME agencies and line ministries), financial authorities, and central banks, as well as dedicated national firm-level surveys to supplement missing data.

Aggregate MSME Data

We use time series country data to estimate three of the five dimensions of Nonfinance Sub-Index (scale of MSMEs, employment, and productivity) and one of the five dimensions of the Finance Sub-Index (financial depth) under the SME-DI. The data cover Brunei Darussalam (2010–2019), Cambodia (2007–2019), Indonesia (2010–2019), the Lao PDR (2006–2019), Malaysia (2003–2019), Myanmar (2006–2019), the Philippines (2006–2019), Singapore (2010–2019), Thailand (2007–2019), and Viet Nam (2007–2019). Ten indicators are extracted from the ADB Asia SME Monitor 2020 database:[11] (i) MSMEs to total enterprises (%), (ii) MSME employees to total workforce (%), (iii) MSME contribution to GDP (%), (iv) MSME bank loans to total bank lending (%), (v) MSME bank loans to country GDP (%), (vi) MSME nonperforming loans to total MSME bank loans (%), (vii) nonbank finance institution (NBFI) financing to bank loans (%), (viii) NBFI financing to country GDP (%), (ix) NBFI nonperforming financing to total financing (%), and (x) market capitalization to country GDP (%) (equity markets that MSMEs can tap). Missing data are calculated based on compound annual growth across all countries (especially MSMEs to total enterprises and MSME employees to total workforce). For bank credit and capital market data, if indicators are unavailable for MSMEs, we use overall banking data (that includes MSME bank credit; for Cambodia, the Lao PDR, and Viet Nam) and main board data (not SME-focused but SMEs tapped; for Cambodia, Indonesia, the Lao PDR, and Myanmar). For the Lao PDR, bank credit data from 2006 to 2014 use the same percentage share of data in 2014.

Granular Enterprise Data

In 2019, we discussed with (i) Credit Bureau Cambodia (CBC), (ii) Department of Enterprise Registration and Management of the Ministry of Industry and Commerce in the Lao PDR, (iii) Credit Bureau Malaysia, (iv) Directorate of Investment and Company Administration in Myanmar, and (v) Agency for Business Registration of the Ministry of Planning and Investment in Viet Nam to use their firm-level data to design the SME-DI (Table 5).

[11]   ADB. 2020 *ADB Asia Small and Medium-Sized Enterprise Monitor Volume 1: Country and Regional Reviews.* https://data.adb.org/dataset/2020-adb-asia-sme-monitor-vol1-country-regional-reviews.

Table 5: Granular Enterprise Data Availability in Select Asian Countries

A. Nonfinance Data

Item	Cambodia		Lao PDR	Myanmar	Viet Nam	Malaysia
	CBC 2019 20,000 samples	CIES 2014 12,155 samples	DERM 2017–2019 32,157 samples	DICA 2017–2019 66,770 samples	ABR 2017–2019 4,785 samples	CBM 2019
	Availability	Availability	Availability	Availability	Availability	Availability
Company name	N	Y	Y	Y	Y	Y
Enterprise code or tax code	Y	Y	Y	Y	Y	Y
Legal form	Y	Y	Y	Y	Y	Y
Company location/address	Y	Y	Y	Y	Y	Y
Establishment date	Y	Y	Y	Y	Y	Y
Main business sector	Y	Y	Y	Y	Y	Y
Number of total employees	Y	Y	N	N	Y	N
% of female employees to total employees	N	Y	N	Y	N	N
Size of company (micro, small, medium, and large firm; classified by the national definition)	Y	Y	N	Y	Y	Y
Company status (registered/liquidation/ bankruptcy)	Y	Y	Y	Y	Y	Y
Charter capital (LCY)	N	N	Y	Y	Y	Y
Average monthly wage per employee (LCY)	N	Y	N	N	N	N
Annual salary per employee (LCY) and annual growth (%)	N	Y	N	N	N	N
Net sales (LCY) and annual growth (%)	N	Y	N	N	Y	Y
Annual turnover/revenue/ profit after tax (LCY), and annual growth (%)	N	Y	N	N	Y	Y

continued on next page

Table 5 continued

B. Finance Data

Item	Cambodia		Lao PDR	Myanmar	Viet Nam	Malaysia
	CBC 2019 20,000 samples	CIES 2014 12,155 samples	DERM 2017–2019 32,157 samples	DICA 2017–2019 66,770 samples	ABR 2017–2019 4,785 samples	CBM 2019
	Availability	Availability	Availability	Availability	Availability	Availability
Loans outstanding from banks:	Y	Y	N	Y	N	Y
of which, loans from state-owned banks	Y	N	N	N	N	N
of which, loans from private sector banks	Y	N	N	N	N	N
of which, guaranteed loans	N	N	N	N	N	N
Loans outstanding from microfinance institutions [MFIs]	Y	N	N	N	N	N
Financing outstanding from leasing companies (LCY)	Y	N	N	N	N	N
Financing outstanding from other financial institutions (LCY)	Y	N	N	N	N	N
Annual borrowing rate (%)	N	N	N	N	N	N
from banks (FCY loans)	N	N	N	N	N	N
from banks (LCY loans)	N	N	N	N	N	N
from MFIs	N	N	N	N	N	N
from others	N	N	N	N	N	N
Type of collateral	Y	N	N	N	N	N
Purpose of the loans	Y	N	N	N	N	N
Loan tenor (year)	Y	N	N	N	N	N
Credit status (completion/ under repayment)	N	N	N	N	N	Y
Payment/overdue condition (days/months of overdue)	Y	N	N	N	N	Y
Past record of credit guarantee implementation (for default)	N	N	N	N	N	N
Past record of loan rejection	N	N	N	N	N	Y

ABR = Agency for Business Registration, CBC = Credit Bureau Cambodia, CBM = Credit Bureau Malaysia, CIES = Cambodia Inter-censal Economic Survey, DERM = Department of Enterprise Registration and Management, DICA = Directorate of Investment and Company Administration, FYC = foreign currency, LCY = local currency.
Note: Y = available, N = not available or alternative data available.
Source: Authors' compilation.

In this report, we use CBC's administrative enterprise data to estimate one of the five dimensions (financial depth) under the Finance Sub-Index of the SME-DI. The data include (i) company profiles denoting company/tax code, legal forms, geographical locations, establishment dates (operating period), main economic sectors, and number of employees; and (ii) credit history data including loans outstanding by commercial banks and NBFIs, loan tenure, type of collateral for loans, and payment/overdue conditions. Total samples included 1,344 firms, of which 1,029 are MSMEs classified by the national definition.[12] CBC also holds individual consumer data of around 20,000 samples including self-employed and sole proprietors; however, we will use this dataset in the second analysis after the test-run with enterprise data as it takes time to separate business data on MSMEs from individual consumers. As the enterprise data are regarded as a technically acceptable sample size for analysis, we conduct the test-run of the two-stage PCA with this dataset to measure the financial depth sub-dimension.

Besides CBC data, we also consider the use of the Cambodia Inter-censal Economic Survey (CIES) data in 2014 for assessing select dimensions of the Nonfinance Sub-Index of the SME-DI.[13] The data cover 12,155 enterprises including both finance and nonfinance data denoting legal forms, gender of the owner, geographic locations, establishment dates (operating period), main economic sectors, number of employees, total monthly/daily revenues/sales and costs (monthly/daily net profit), and loans from banks and other external parties; however, as loan data are mostly blank, we will use nonfinance data to measure select dimensions of the Nonfinance Sub-Index. As the CIES 2019 was launched in August 2020, the analysis of the CIES will not be covered in this report.

Box 2: Profile of MSMEs Registered in Credit Bureau Cambodia

Micro, small and medium-sized enterprises (MSMEs) registered in Credit Bureau Cambodia (CBC) mostly operate in capital city Phnom Penh (78.5% of the total enterprises registered) (Annex). Around one-third of the MSMEs were young companies operating for 5 years or less (33.5%). By business sector, retail and wholesale trade accounted for 28%, followed by construction (14.6%), other services (10.4%), real estate (9.7%), and manufacturing (8.6%). A majority of MSMEs (63.7%) employed 10-50 workers.

Loans outstanding (average of plural loans) by MSMEs amounted to $2.2 million, less than one-third of large firms. However, it is a relatively large amount for the segment of MSMEs, which may be due to sectors such as construction and real estate. Around half of MSMEs raised funds to finance working capital, while only 6% did for investment capital (loans for construction and the purchase of machinery and heavy equipment), with the remaining doing so for other purposes, including buying assets (real estate). There were 78.1% of MSMEs with access to mid- to long-term loans (42.1% for mid-term [13–59 months] and 36.4% for long-term [60 months and more] loans).

Collateral was required for 75% of MSMEs in the form of immovable assets, 13.4% used movable assets such as vehicles and inventory for loans, and 16.1% received unsecured loans. A small portion of MSMEs used corporate guarantees for loans (1.9%). There were 85% of MSMEs with overdue loans (past due of up to 89 days for long-term loans and up to 30 days for short-term loans), but these were still classified as performing loans. There were 34.8% completed loan repayments (closed). Only 3.7% of MSMEs had nonperforming loans (substandard, doubtful, and loss; past due of over 90 days for long-term loans and over 31 days for short-term loans). Only a tiny fraction (0.5%) was able to write-off loans.

---

[12]   According to the Small and Medium Enterprise Development Framework of Cambodia (2015), microenterprise refers to the firm with assets of $50,000 and below and a fewer than 10 employees; small enterprise refers to the firm with assets $50,000–$250,000 and 10–50 employees; medium-sized enterprise refers to the firm with assets $250,000–$500,000 and 51–100 employees.

[13]   ADB received individual enterprise data of CIES 2014 in collaboration with the National Institute of Statistics under the Ministry of Planning in Cambodia.

Estimation Results

By using the two datasets, we conduct the test-run of the two-stage PCA to measure selected dimensions for the regional and country (Cambodia) SME-DI. The main objective of this exercise is to test the feasibility of SME-DI and extract issues to improve and develop the index.

1. Regional SME Development Index Exercise Based on Aggregate MSME Data

First-Stage Principal Component Analysis

This exercise based on aggregate MSME data with time series focuses on three dimensions of the Nonfinance Sub-Index (scale of MSMEs, employment, and productivity) and one dimension of the Finance Sub-Index (financial depth) under the SME-DI. Due to limited data availability, we restructured and simplified factors affecting MSME development into four dimensions: (i) macro conditions, (ii) bank financing, (iii) nonbank financing, and (iv) equity financing (Figure 1).

For the first stage, we organize the 12 variables into four likely factors. Indicators on "inflation" and "lending rate" are extracted from International Monetary Fund/International Financial Statistics (IMF/IFS) end-of-year time series data. Other indicators are explained in the abovementioned "data selection."

- Macro conditions (Macro): Number of MSMEs to total number of firms ("num"), MSME employees to total employees ("emp"), MSME contribution to GDP ("gdp", and the annual inflation rate ("inf").
- Bank financing (Bank): MSME bank loans to total ("bkc"), MSME bank loans to GDP ("bkc_gdp"), MSME nonperforming loans to total MSME bank loans ("bkc_npl", and commercial bank lending rate ("len_r").
- Nonbank financing (Nonbank): NBFI financing to total bank loans ("nbkc"), NBFI financing to GDP ("nbkc_gdp"), and NBFI nonperforming loans to total NBFI financing ("nbkc_npl").
- Equity financing (Equity): Market capitalization to GDP ("m_cap").

In equation form, we have the following (Huh and Park, 2017):

$$Z(a)_i = \alpha_{i1}Xa_{i1} + \alpha_{i2}Xa_{i2} + \alpha_{i3}Xa_{i3} + \alpha_{i4}Xa_{i4} \qquad (3)$$

where $Z(a)_i$ is the i th principal component on macro conditions *(Macro)*, Xa_1 the number of MSMEs to total number of firms ("num"), Xa_2 denotes MSME employees to total employees ("emp"), Xa_3 denotes MSME contribution to GDP ("gdp"), and Xa_4 is inflation ("inf").

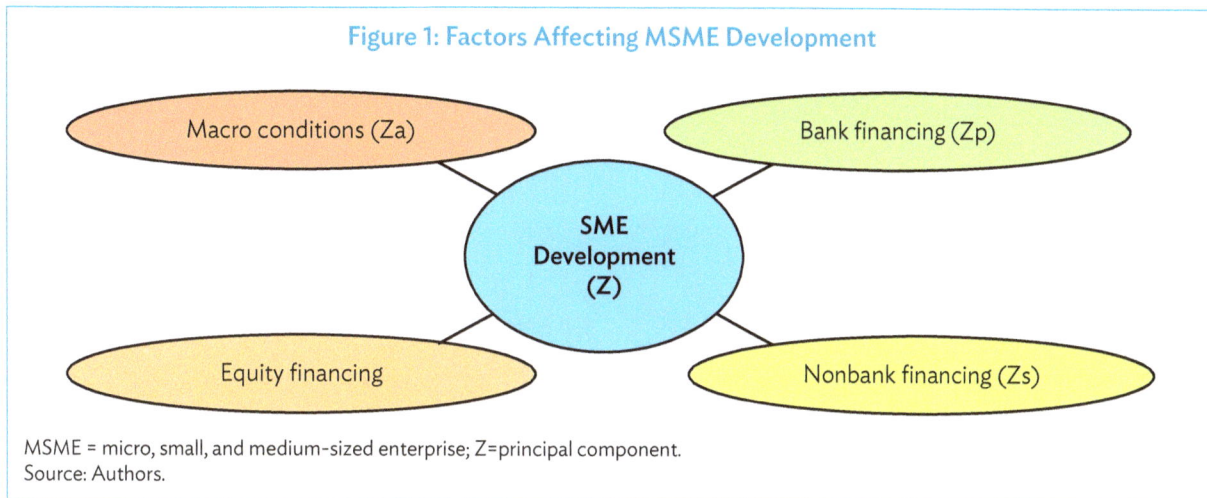

Figure 1: Factors Affecting MSME Development

MSME = micro, small, and medium-sized enterprise; Z=principal component.
Source: Authors.

$$Z(p)_i = \beta_{i1}Xp_{i1} + \beta_{i2}Xp_{i2} + \beta_{i3}Xp_{i3} + \beta_{i4}Xp_{i4} \qquad (4)$$

where $Z(p)_i$ is the ith principal component on bank financing (*Bank*), Xp_1 denotes MSME bank loans to total ("bkc"), Xp_2 denotes MSME bank loans to GDP ("bkc_gdp"), Xp_3 denotes MSME nonperforming loans to total MSME bank loans ("bkc_npl"), and Xp_4 is the commercial bank lending rate ("len_r").

$$Z(s)_i = \gamma_{i1}Xs_{i1} + \gamma_{i2}Xs_{i2} + \gamma_{i3}Xs_{i3} \qquad (5)$$

where $Z(s)_i$ is the ith principal component on nonbank financing (*Nonbank*), Xs_1 denotes NBFI financing to total bank loans ("nbkc"), Xs_2 denotes NBFI financing to GDP ("nbkc_gdp"), and Xs_3 denotes NBFI nonperforming loans to total NBFI financing ("nbkc_npl").

Table 6 shows eigenvalues of each component under each indicator (dimension)—*Macro* (D1), *Bank* (D2), and *Nonbank* (D3). Based on the results, we use the first two components for each dimension. Each eigenvalue is 0.95 or higher, with the exception of "emp" in D1 which has an eigenvalue of only 0.70. Because it adds another 0.17 to the cumulative, raising it from 0.69 to 0.86, we opted to include it in the analysis.

Table 6: Results of Principal Component Analysis, Regional SME-DI (First Stage)

Dimension	Component	Eigenvalue	Proportion	Cumulative
D1: Macro (74 obs)	PC1: num	2.7486	0.6872	0.6872
	PC2: emp	0.6956	0.1739	0.8611
	PC3: gdp	0.4098	0.1025	0.9635
	PC4: inf	0.1458	0.0365	1.0000
D2: Bank (88 obs)	PC1: bkc	1.9227	0.4807	0.4807
	PC2: bkc_gdp	1.4070	0.3517	0.8324
	PC3: bkc_npl	0.5475	0.1369	0.9693
	PC4: len_r	0.1227	0.0307	1.0000
D3: Nonbank (60 obs.)	PC1: nbkc	1.8417	0.6139	0.6139
	PC2: nbkc_gdp	0.9526	0.3176	0.9315
	PC3: nbkc_npl	0.2056	0.0685	1.0000

obs = observation, SME-DI = Small and Medium-Sized Enterprise Development Index.
Source: Calculation based on ADB Asia SME Monitor 2020 database.

From this, by dimension, we calculated squared loadings of each variable in the selected principal components $(Z_1, Z_2,..., Z_i)$ (Table 7).

Table 7: Squared Loadings, Regional SME-DI (First Stage)

Dimension	Z_1	Z_2
D1: Macro (74 obs.)		
PC1: num	0.7044	0.0008
PC2: emp	0.7567	0.1100
PC3: gdp	0.8495	0.0555
PC4: inf	0.4381	0.5294
D2: Bank (88 obs.)		
PC1: bkc	0.9206	0.0003
PC2: bkc_gdp	0.6524	0.0839
PC3: bkc_npl	0.0514	0.7467
PC4: len_r	0.2983	0.5761
D3: Nonbank (60 obs.)		
PC1: nbkc	0.8709	0.0264
PC2: nbkc_gdp	0.8727	0.0244
PC3: nbkc_npl	0.0980	0.9019

obs = observation, SME-DI = Small and Medium-Sized Enterprise Development Index.
Source: Calculation based on ADB Asia SME Monitor 2020 database.

The sum of squared loadings in each Z_i is λ ($\lambda_1, \lambda_2,... \lambda_i$). We calculated θ as the proportion of respective λ ($\lambda_1, \lambda_2,... \lambda_i$) to the total λ ($\lambda_1 + \lambda_2 + ...+ \lambda_i$). Then, "squared loadings to the unity sum (η)" (Huh and Park, 2017) were calculated as the proportion of the squared loading to the λ in each component (Z_i). In the next step, we calculated weights of respective variables of the dimension as the sum of "η by θ" of each component (Z_i). Table 8 shows the weights (scores) of each dimension obtained through the first-stage PCA.

Table 8: Weights for Index, Regional SME-DI (First Stage)

Dimension	Weight
Macro	
PC1: num-MSMEs to total (%)	0.2047
PC2: emp-MSME employees to total (%)	0.2516
PC3: gdp-MSME contribution to GDP (%)	0.2627
PC4: inf-Annual inflation rate (%)	0.2809
Bank	
PC1: bkc-MSME bank loans to total (%)	0.2766
PC2: bkc_gdp-MSME bank loans to GDP (%)	0.2211
PC3: bkc_npl-MSME nonperforming loans to total MSME bank loans	0.2397
PC4: len_r-Annual commercial bank lending rate (%)	0.2626
Nonbank	
PC1: nbkc-NBFI financing to bank loans (%)	0.3211
PC2: nbkc_gdp-NBFI financing to GDP (%)	0.3210
PC3: nbkc_npl-NBFI nonperforming loans to total NBFI financing	0.3579

GDP = gross domestic product; MSME = micro, small, and medium-sized enterprise; NBFI = nonbank finance institution; SME-DI = Small and Medium-Sized Enterprise Development Index.
Source: Calculation based on ADB Asia SME Monitor 2020 database.

Note that there is only one variable, market_cap, for equity financing (*Equity*). We insert it in the second stage of the PCA.

Second-Stage Principal Component Analysis

Referring to Table 9, we calculate eigenvalues in the overall index as the aggregation of four dimensions (*Macro, Bank, Nonbank, and Equity*). As the first two components accounted for 89.7% of the variance and had eigenvalues of 1.45 or higher, we used these two components for the second-stage PCA. Similar to the first-stage PCA, we compute squared loadings two components (Z_1 and Z_2) (Table 10). We then calculate weights for each dimension following the same path of analysis as in the first-stage PCA (Table 11).

Table 9: Results of Principal Component Analysis, Regional SME-DI (Second Stage) with Four Dimensions

Dimension (75 obs.)	Eigenvalue	Proportion	Cumulative
Macro	2.1299	0.5325	0.5325
Bank	1.4579	0.3645	0.8969
Nonbank	0.2552	0.0638	0.9608
Equity	0.1570	0.0392	1.0000

obs = observation, SME-DI = Small and Medium-Sized Enterprise Development Index.
Source: Calculation based on ADB Asia SME Monitor 2020 database.

Table 10: Squared Loadings, Regional SME-DI (Second Stage) with Four Dimensions

Dimension (75 obs.)	Z_1	Z_2
D1: Macro	0.7262	0.1909
D2: Bank	0.6048	0.2635
D3: Nonbank	0.3723	0.5057
D4: Equity	0.4265	0.4979

obs = observation, SME-DI = Small and Medium-Sized Enterprise Development Index.
Source: Calculation based on ADB Asia SME Monitor 2020 database.

Table 11: Weights for Index, Regional SME-DI (Second Stage) with Four Dimensions

Dimension (75 obs.)	Weight
D1: Macro	0.2556
D2: Bank	0.2420
D3: Nonbank	0.2447
D4: Equity	0.2577

obs = observation, SME-DI = Small and Medium-Sized Enterprise Development Index.
Source: Calculation based on ADB Asia SME Monitor 2020 database.

In the second stage, it is necessary to drop the NBFI variable from the Nonbank dimension to have enough observations to perform the analysis. Doing so yields the results above. From this aggregate data, we can estimate the index using a weight of 25.56% on the macro conditions, 24.20% for bank financing, 24.47% for nonbank financing, and 25.77% for equity. As a robustness check, we offer another version of the second stage with only the first three dimensions. We do this because the fourth dimension (Equity) comprises just one variable whereas the others comprise several variables. While it is sensible to use all available data in our model, it is unusual that a dimension contains just one variable. In future, we expect to have more Equity data so it consists of several variables like the others. For the second-stage PCA with three dimensions, we employed the same methods described previously (Tables 12, 13, 14). In this version, we include the m_cap variable in Nonbank and do not use the nbkc_npl variable in the estimate.

Table 12: Results of Principal Component Analysis, Regional SME-DI (Second Stage) with Three Dimensions

Dimension (61 obs.)	Eigenvalue	Proportion	Cumulative
Macro	2.0502	0.6834	0.6834
Bank	0.8271	0.2757	0.9591
Nonbank	0.1226	0.0409	1.0000

obs = observation, SME-DI = Small and Medium-Sized Enterprise Development Index.
Source: Calculation based on ADB Asia SME Monitor 2020 database.

The first two components have eigenvalues of 0.8 or higher and account for 91.8% of the variance. The squared loadings and weights are:

Table 13: Squared Loadings, Regional SME-DI (Second Stage) with Three Dimensions

Dimension (61 obs.)	Z_1	Z_2
D1: Macro	0.2976	0.7016
D2: Bank	0.8527	0.0888
D3: Nonbank	0.8998	0.0367

obs = observation, SME-DI = Small and Medium-Sized Enterprise Development Index.
Source: Calculation based on ADB Asia SME Monitor 2020 database.

Table 14: Weights for Index, Regional SME-DI (Second Stage) with Three Dimensions

Item			All	
Dimension 1 -Macro conditions			Weights	0.3473
1a	Number of MSMEs to total firms	value	0.2047	
1b	Number of MSME employees to total employees	value	0.2516	
1c	MSME contribution to GDP	value	0.2627	
1d	Annual inflation rate	value	0.2809	

continued on next page

Table 14 continued

Item			All	
Dimension 2 –Bank financing			Weights	0.3272
2a	MSME bank loans to total bank loans	value	0.2766	
2b	MSME bank loans to GDP	value	0.2211	
2c	MSME nonperforming loans to total MSME bank loans	value	0.2397	
2d	Annual commercial bank lending rate	value	0.2626	
Dimension 3 –Nonbank financing			Weights	0.3255
3a	NBFI financing to total bank loans	value	0.3232	
3b	NBFI financing to GDP	value	0.3231	
3c	Equity financing–Market capitalization to GDP	value	0.3537	
Overall				1.0000

GDP = gross domestic product; MSME = micro, small, and medium enterprise; NBFI = nonbank finance institution; SME-DI = Small and Medium-Sized Enterprise Development Index.
Note: number of observations: (all) 61.
Source: Calculation based on ADB Asia SME Monitor 2020 database.

These results suggest that when estimating the SME-DI using aggregate data, we weigh the macroeconomic factors 34.73%, the bank financing 32.72%, and the nonbank financing 32.55%. Compared with the four-dimensional estimate of the SME-DI, these results seem more plausible given the eigenvalues and proportion explained by the Macro and Bank dimensions; however, the fourth dimension (Equity) is forward-looking in that as we refine the SME-DI we will collect more data on this important dimension. For this reason, we present both models as the three-dimensional estimate is more credible given the current country-level, while the four-dimensional model represents our future direction.

Taking the current model of three dimensions, the results indicate that macro conditions such as the contribution of MSMEs to total number of firms, employment, and productivity are the most important predictors of SME development. When allocating scarce resources to improve SME development, policymakers should focus on these macro conditions first. Financing remains significant, though whether MSMEs access it through the banking sector or through the nonbank finance sector is less important given the relatively equal weights of the two in the model. While Bank dimension is higher, it is not significantly so. On the other hand, the Bank dimension has a much higher eigenvalue and proportion than the Nonbank dimension. These findings suggest that policymakers can approach the issue of MSME access in two fundamental ways: (i) continue training programs for MSMEs in financial literacy so they can be more successful in obtaining bank loans, and (ii) develop further the NBFI sector as, in general, it is easier for MSMEs to secure financing from NBFIs than from banks. Since both channels remain important, policymakers need to keep both in mind.

We present the results of the regional SME-DI exercise using aggregate data in Figure 2.

Figure 2: Three Dimensions of the Regional SME-DI

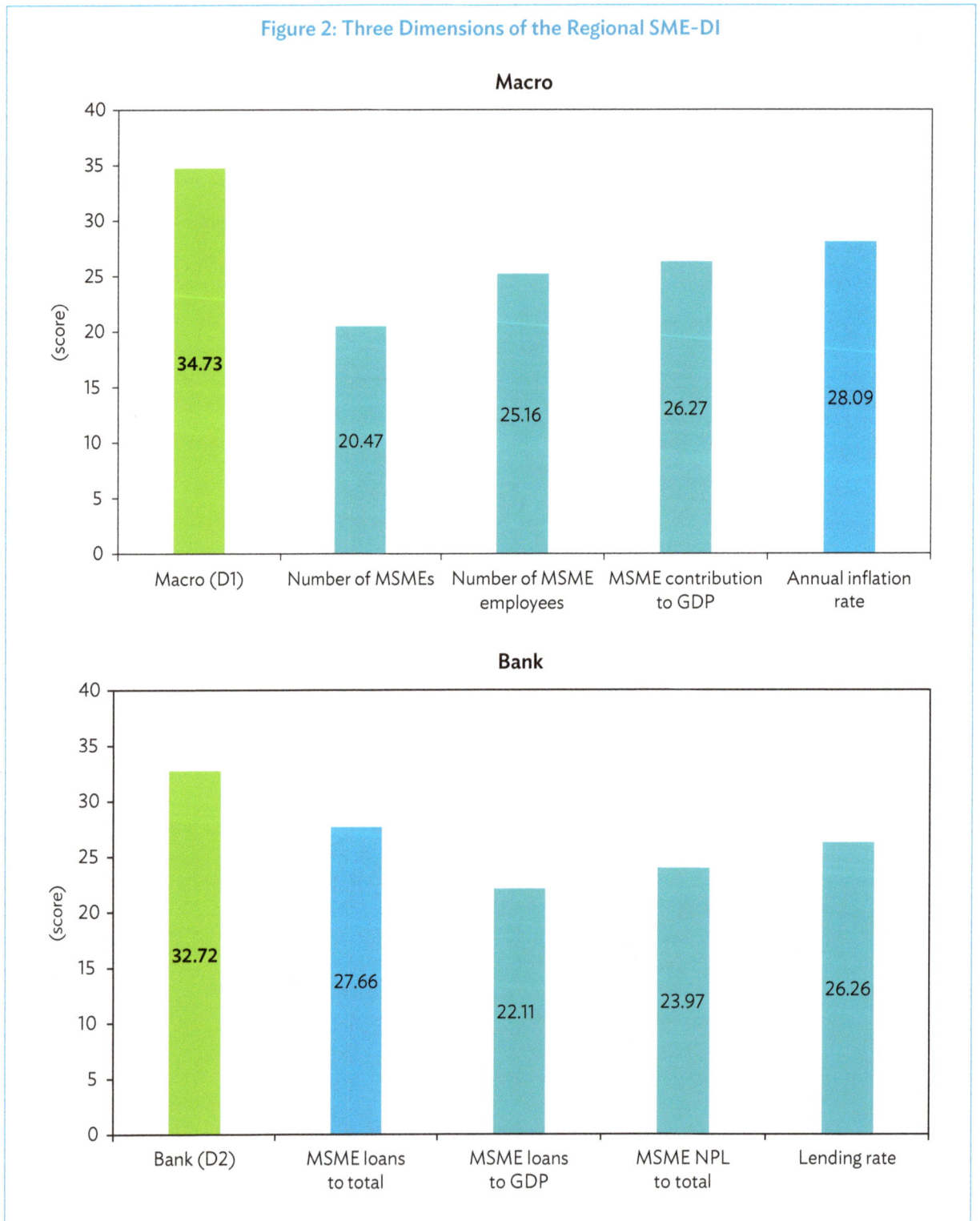

Macro

Bank

continued on next page

Figure 2 continued

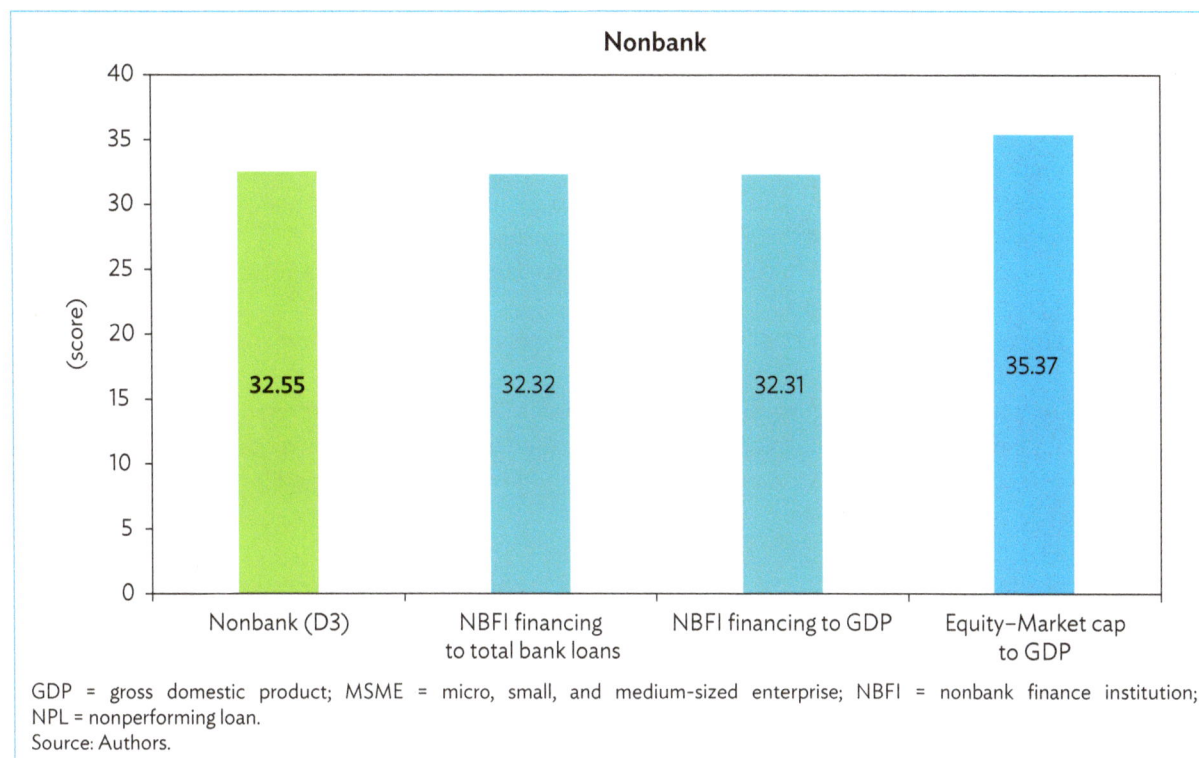

GDP = gross domestic product; MSME = micro, small, and medium-sized enterprise; NBFI = nonbank finance institution; NPL = nonperforming loan.
Source: Authors.

2.   Country SME Development Index Exercise Based on Granular Enterprise Data

This exercise is based on firm-level data captured by CBC to design the country index. Generally, MSMEs registered with CBC seem to have healthy funding conditions (Box 2). This section investigates their performance in detail through the PCA test-run to measure the financial depth dimension of the Finance Sub-Index at the country level (as a sample case).

Overall Principal Component Analysis for MSMEs

First, we conducted an overall PCA for MSMEs, using all available data items of the CBC enterprise dataset. The objective of overall PCA is to observe the characteristics of MSMEs registered with CBC and extract variable groups to generate three indicators—*Access, Products, and Soundness*—under the financial depth dimension of the Finance Sub-Index.

Table 15 shows the results of the overall PCA for MSMEs. The first 10 components have an eigenvalue of 1.0 or higher and cumulatively explain 75% of all MSMEs registered with CBC. A higher weight indicates a higher impact of the component in the range between zero and 1. Each component illustrates the following:

- Component 1: group of MSMEs taking local currency bank loans but having a relatively high level of past due amount for a duration of up to 89 days, and filling their funding gap from microfinance institutions (MFIs).
- Component 2: group of MSMEs taking USD-denominated bank loans but having a relatively high level of past due amount for a duration of up to 89 days.

- Component 3: group of MSMEs taking loans from state-owned banks.
- Component 4: group of MSMEs accessing relatively longer-term bank loans.
- Component 5: group of relatively small MSMEs such as sole proprietors (negative weight) located in urban areas,[14] including the capital city, Phnom Penh.
- Component 6: group of MSMEs taking loans for working capital (negative weight) and other purposes.
- Component 7: group of MSMEs with a relatively longer operating period.
- Component 8: group of MSMEs taking loans for investment purposes.
- Component 9: group of MSMEs in specific sectors such as trade with a relatively small number of employees (negative weight).
- Component 10: group of MSMEs with higher USD-denominated nonperforming loans (NPLs).

Based on this result, the factors affecting the financial depth of MSMEs can be interpreted as follows (Figure 3): (i) local currency bank loans and MFI loans, (ii) USD-denominated bank loans, (iii) loans from state-owned banks, (iv) past due conditions and NPLs, (v) loan tenor, (vi) loan purpose, (vii) firm size and location, (viii) operating period, and (ix) sector and employment.

Referring to these factors, we extract the variables to be used for the first-stage PCA for estimating three indicators (*Access, Products, and Soundness*). Trade finance data are not utilized as variables for the analysis as these are not influential to most of the components (Table 15). Among the factors mentioned above, variables on location, operating period, and economic sector are not used in this test-run. These will be used as dummy or category variables in the next analysis, together with necessary improvements of analytical models.

Table 15: Overall Principal Component Analysis, MSMEs in Cambodia

Variable	Comp1	Comp2	Comp3	Comp4	Comp5	Comp6	Comp7	Comp8	Comp9	Comp10	Comp11	Comp12	Comp13	Unexplained
lf	0.0292	-0.0388	-0.0324	0.0019	-0.6569	0.0481	0.0416	-0.0513	0.1132	-0.0788	0.0008	-0.1094	-0.0154	0.2983
l_b	0.0013	-0.0126	-0.0402	-0.0392	0.681	0.0587	-0.0581	0.0104	0.1615	0.1014	0.0321	-0.0453	0.0187	0.2817
op	0.0379	-0.1351	0.0025	0.086	-0.0587	0.0031	0.8974	0.1134	-0.1016	0.0587	0.0703	0.025	0.0036	0.1827
sec	0.0485	-0.0903	0.017	0.0644	0.2422	-0.0327	0.009	-0.0014	0.6599	-0.2461	-0.0287	-0.0691	-0.0552	0.3335
emp_num	-0.0056	0.065	-0.0041	-0.0731	0.1788	-0.0088	0.2811	-0.0773	-0.6242	-0.1957	-0.0885	-0.0932	-0.044	0.2795
bl_ls	0.0027	-0.0023	0.7064	-0.0085	-0.0152	-0.0162	-0.0001	-0.0019	0.0347	0.0086	0.0049	-0.0035	0.0024	0.05151
bl_us	-0.0033	0.0052	0.703	-0.001	0.0046	0.0201	0.0033	-0.0084	-0.0155	0.0021	-0.0003	-0.0041	0.0003	0.05262
bl_lp	0.4998	0.0155	-0.0055	-0.0157	-0.0073	-0.0071	0.0206	-0.0064	0.0114	0.0084	-0.0061	0.0031	0.0056	0.01755
bl_up	0.0281	0.6703	-0.0356	0.0563	0.0224	-0.0011	-0.1086	0.0382	-0.0615	0.009	0.0545	-0.0082	-0.008	0.05421
tf_l	0.0046	-0.0091	0.0019	0.0017	0.022	-0.0013	0.0033	0.0108	-0.0122	-0.0272	-0.0075	-0.011	0.9962	0.006136
tf_u	-0.0785	0.3003	-0.0097	-0.2163	-0.0983	-0.0057	0.2926	-0.0421	0.364	0.0723	-0.0766	0.0133	0.0103	0.3675
mfi_l	0.4977	0.0153	-0.0062	-0.0058	-0.0098	0.0093	0.02	-0.0032	0.0146	0.0114	-0.005	0.0054	-0.0011	0.02757
mfi_f	0.4946	0.0233	-0.0061	-0.0146	-0.012	0.0077	0.0183	0.0012	0.0151	0.0118	-0.0037	0.0051	-0.0011	0.03244
lp_wc	0.0032	0.0334	-0.0142	0.027	0.0329	-0.6883	0.0863	-0.215	0.0265	-0.0134	0.0274	0.0001	0.0394	0.1698
lp_inv	-0.0077	0.0497	-0.0071	-0.0167	0.0408	-0.01	0.1185	0.9557	0.0383	-0.0377	-0.0135	-0.0158	0.0109	0.05455
lp_ot	0.0042	0.0286	-0.0092	0.0243	0.0425	0.7184	0.0809	-0.2037	-0.0038	-0.0315	0.0208	0.0027	0.0334	0.1515
lt_av	-0.0067	0.0012	-0.0211	0.6954	-0.0826	-0.0349	-0.0422	-0.0021	-0.0051	0.0123	-0.0133	-0.0298	-0.0044	0.1708

continued on next page

---

[14] CBC defines "urban" as all districts in Phnom Penh (municipality district is referred to the urban district of each of 24 provinces) and "rural" as all districts excluded the municipality district in each of 24 provinces, not including Phnom Penh.

Table 15 continued

Variable	Comp1	Comp2	Comp3	Comp4	Comp5	Comp6	Comp7	Comp8	Comp9	Comp10	Comp11	Comp12	Comp13	Unexplained
lt_lng	-0.0329	0.1057	0.014	0.6809	0.0438	0.0406	0.1973	-0.0273	0.1074	0.0174	-0.032	0.0271	0.0081	0.1762
ocpl_lcy	0.4998	0.0141	0.0166	-0.0144	-0.0076	-0.0075	0.0194	-0.0082	0.0128	0.0083	-0.0062	0.0028	0.0056	0.0181
ocpl_fcy	0.0284	0.6678	0.0403	0.0571	0.0136	0.0007	-0.1167	0.0391	-0.0627	-0.0474	0.0037	-0.0051	-0.0059	0.05241
ocnpl_lcy	0.008	-0.0082	-0.0053	-0.0055	0.0362	0.0019	0.0263	-0.0167	0.0088	-0.0471	-0.0104	0.9867	-0.0109	0.0205
ocnpl_fcy	0.0191	-0.0193	0.0073	0.0177	0.1179	-0.0143	0.0647	-0.0379	-0.0417	0.9469	-0.0278	-0.0468	-0.027	0.09405
ocwo_tot	-0.0101	0.0339	0.0032	-0.0287	0.0206	-0.0027	0.0715	-0.0148	0.0192	-0.0277	0.9926	-0.0103	-0.0074	0.01738

lf= legal forms (sole proprietorship, general partnership, limited partnership, private limited company, public limited company, branch of a foreign company, commercial representative office of a foreign company, cooperative, state-owned organization, non-governmental organization, and others), l_b=location (urban or rural), op=operating period (0-5] years,]5-10] years,]10-15] years,]15-30] years, and]30 years and above), sec=economic sector (agriculture, mining, manufacturing, utilities, construction, trade, finance, transport, IT, other services, real estate, and others), emp_num=number of employees, bl_ls=bank loans outstanding (local currency) from state-owned bank, bl_us=bank loans outstanding (US$) from state-owned bank, bl_lp=bank loans outstanding (local currency) from private sector banks, bl_up= bank loans outstanding (US$) from state-owned bank, tf_l=trade finance (local currency), tf_u=trade finance (US$), mfi_l=loans (local currency) from microfinance institutions (MFIs), mfi_f=loans (US$) from MFIs, lp_wc=loan purpose (working capital), lp_inv=loan purpose (investment capital), lp_ot=loan purpose (others), lt_av=loan tenor (average of plural loans; 1-12 months [short-term loans], 13-59 months [mid-term loans], and 60 months and more [long-term loans]), lt_lng=loan tenor (the longest among plural loans), ocpl_lcy=overdue condition (performing loans, local currency), ocpl_fcy=overdue condition (performing loans, US$), ocnpl_lcy=overdue condition (nonperforming loans [NPLs], local currency), ocnpl_fcy=overdue condition (NPLs, US$), ocwo_tot=overdue condition (write-off, total), MSME=micro, small, and medium-sized enterprise.

Note: Promax rotated components.

Source: Calculations based on administrative enterprise data from Credit Bureau Cambodia, 2019.

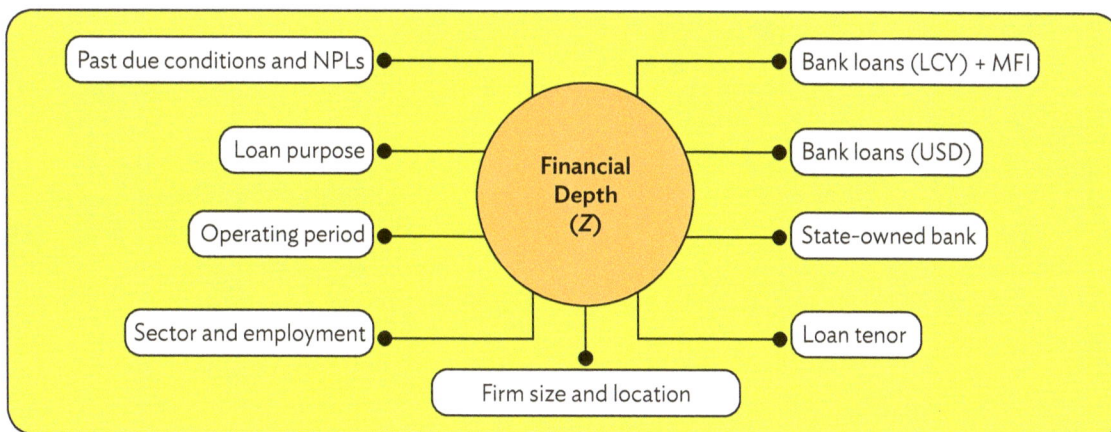

Figure 3: Factors Affecting the Financial Depth of MSMEs, Cambodia

LCY = local currency; MFI = microfinance institution; MSME = micro, small, and medium-sized enterprise; NPL = nonperforming loan; USD = United States dollar; Z = principal component.

Source: Authors.

First-Stage Principal Component Analysis

Taking account of the result of overall PCA and the number of observations for each variable, we formulated three indicators as follows, referring to the concept of two-stage PCA:

$$Z(a)_i = \alpha_{i1}Xa_{i1} + \alpha_{i2}Xa_{i2} + \alpha_{i3}Xa_{i3} + \alpha_{i4}Xa_{i4} + \alpha_{i5}Xa_{i5} \qquad (1)$$

where $Z(a)_i$ is the ith principal component on access to finance (*Access*), Xa_1 denotes bank loans outstanding from state-owned banks (total of local currency and USD-denominated loans, amounts converted to a single currency USD with the exchange rate of KR4,000/\$1), Xa_2 denotes bank loans outstanding from private sector banks (local currency loans), Xa_3 denotes bank loans outstanding from private sector banks (USD-denominated loans), Xa_4 denotes MFI loans (local currency loans), Xa_5 denotes MFI loans outstanding (USD-denominated loans), and α is weight of each variable.

$$Z(p)_i = \beta_{i1}Xp_{i1} + \beta_{i2}Xp_{i2} + \beta_{i3}Xp_{i3} + \beta_{i4}Xp_{i4} + \beta_{i5}Xp_{i5} + \beta_{i6}Xp_{i6} + \beta_{i7}Xp_{i7} + \beta_{i8}Xp_{i8} + \beta_{i9}Xp_{i9} \qquad (2)$$

where $Z(p)_i$ is the ith principal component on loan products denoted by collateral requirements, loan purpose, and loan tenor (*Products*), Xp_1 denotes non-collateral loans, Xp_2 denotes loans requiring immovable assets (land title), Xp_3 denotes loans requiring movable assets (vehicles and inventory), Xp_4 denotes loans requiring corporate guarantees, Xp_5 denotes loans requiring other collateral, Xp_6 denotes loans for the purpose of working capital, Xp_7 denotes loans for investment capital (loans for construction and purchasing machinery and heavy equipment), Xp_8 denotes loans for other purposes (including loans for buying assets), Xp_9 denotes loan tenor (average of plural loans by firm (1–12 months as short-term loans, 13–59 months as midterm loans, and 60 months and more as long-term loans), and β is weight of each variable.

$$Z(s)_i = \gamma_{i1}Xs_{i1} + \gamma_{i2}Xs_{i2} + \gamma_{i3}Xs_{i3} + \gamma_{i4}Xs_{i4} + \gamma_{i5}Xs_{i5} \qquad (3)$$

where $Z(s)_i$ is the ith principal component on the soundness of the loan (*Soundness*), Xs_1 denotes local currency loans with past due of up to 89 days for long-term loans and up to 30 days for short-term loans (as performing loans), Xs_2 denotes USD-denominated loans as performing loans, Xs_3 denotes local currency loans with past due of over 90 days for long-term loans and over 31 days for short-term loans (as NPLs combining substandard, doubtful, and loss), Xs_4 denotes USD-denominated loans as NPLs, Xs_5 denotes write-off balance of the loan, and γ is weight of each variable.

Table 16 shows the eigenvalues of each component under each indicator (dimension)—*Access* (D1), *Products* (D2), and *Soundness* (D3). Based on the result, we use first 3 components for D1, 5 components for D2, and 4 components for D3, given the eigenvalue of around 1.0 or higher. From the foregoing result, by dimension, we calculated squared loadings of each variable in the selected principal components ($Z_1, Z_2,... Z_i$) (Table 17).

The sum of squared loadings in each Z_i is λ ($\lambda_1, \lambda_2,... \lambda_i$). θ was calculated as the proportion of respective λ ($\lambda_1, \lambda_2,... \lambda_i$) to the total λ ($\lambda_1 + \lambda_2 +...+ \lambda_i$). Then, "squared loadings to the unity sum (η)" were calculated as the proportion of the squared loading to the λ in each component (Z_i). Then, weights of respective variables of the dimension were calculated as the sum of "η by θ" of each component (Z_i). Table 18 shows the weights (scores) of each dimension obtained through the first-stage PCA.

Table 16: Results of Principal Components Analysis, Finance Sub-Index (Financial Depth), Cambodia

Dimension	Component	All (obs=1,344)			MSMEs (obs=1,029)			Large firms (obs=315)		
		Eigenvalue	Proportion	Cumulative	Eigenvalue	Proportion	Cumulative	Eigenvalue	Proportion	Cumulative
D1	PC1	2.6990	0.5398	0.5398	3.1401	0.6280	0.6280	2.4717	0.4943	0.4943
	PC2	1.0002	0.2000	0.7398	1.0002	0.2000	0.8281	1.0019	0.2004	0.6947
	PC3	0.8755	0.1751	0.9149	0.7953	0.1591	0.9871	0.9324	0.1865	0.8812
	PC4	0.3449	0.0690	0.9839	0.3899	0.0078	0.9949	0.4926	0.0985	0.9797
	PC5	0.0804	0.0161	1.0000	0.2545	0.0051	1.0000	0.1014	0.0203	1.0000
D2	PC1	2.0286	0.2254	0.2254	2.0988	0.2332	0.2332	1.8616	0.2068	0.2068
	PC2	0.3600	0.1511	0.3765	1.2745	0.1416	0.3748	1.5389	0.1710	0.3778
	PC3	1.1764	0.1307	0.5072	1.1863	0.1318	0.5066	1.2643	0.1405	0.5183
	PC4	1.0203	0.1134	0.6206	1.0637	0.1182	0.6248	0.9920	0.1102	0.6285
	PC5	0.9408	0.1045	0.7251	0.9859	0.1095	0.7344	0.8550	0.0950	0.7235
	PC6	0.8414	0.0935	0.8186	0.8643	0.0960	0.8304	0.8451	0.0939	0.8174
	PC7	0.7390	0.0821	0.9007	0.7430	0.0826	0.9129	0.7166	0.0796	0.8970
	PC8	0.5971	0.0663	0.9671	0.5019	0.0558	0.9687	0.6071	0.0675	0.9645
	PC9	0.2965	0.0329	1.0000	0.2817	0.0313	1.0000	0.3195	0.0035	1.0000
D3	PC1	1.2971	0.2594	0.2594	1.3857	0.2771	0.2771	1.2501	0.2500	0.2500
	PC2	1.0098	0.2020	0.4614	1.0042	0.2008	0.4780	1.2075	0.2415	0.4915
	PC3	0.9993	0.1999	0.6612	1.0012	0.2002	0.6782	0.9988	0.1998	0.6913
	PC4	0.9909	0.1982	0.8594	0.9938	0.1988	0.8770	0.7936	0.1587	0.8500
	PC5	0.7029	0.1406	1.0000	0.6151	0.1230	1.0000	0.7500	0.1500	1.0000
Overall	PC1	2.0521	0.6840	0.6840	2.0463	0.6821	0.6821	2.0220	0.6740	0.6740
	PC2	0.9420	0.3140	0.9980	0.9512	0.3170	0.9991	0.9695	0.3232	0.9972
	PC3	0.0059	0.0020	1.0000	0.0026	0.0009	1.0000	0.0085	0.0028	1.0000

D1=dimension (indicator) *Access*, D2=dimension *Products*, D3=dimension *Soundness*, PC=principal component.
Source: Calculations based on administrative enterprise data from Credit Bureau Cambodia, 2019.

Table 17: Squared Loadings, Finance Sub-Index (Financial Depth), Cambodia

	All					MSMEs					Large firms				
	Z1	Z2	Z3	Z4	Z5	Z1	Z2	Z3	Z4	Z5	Z1	Z2	Z3	Z4	Z5
D1	0.9718	0.0253				0.9771	0.0217				0.9815	0.0142			
1a	0.0001	0.9982	0.0018			0.0000	0.9994	0.0007			0.0007	0.9677	0.0315		
1b	0.8813	0.0001	0.0239			0.9512	0.0000	0.0227			0.8492	0.0015	0.0270		
1c	0.1999	0.0017	0.7933			0.2741	0.0007	0.7252			0.1462	0.0288	0.8026		
1d	0.8669	0.0002	0.0549			0.9559	0.0001	0.0253			0.8420	0.0038	0.0671		
1e	0.7506	0.0000	0.0016			0.9588	0.0001	0.0213			0.6336	0.0000	0.0041		
D2	0.1073	0.8928				0.0913	0.9086				0.0585	0.9415			
2a	0.2292	0.1153	0.3544	0.0072	0.0541	0.2164	0.1330	0.4062	0.0375	0.0051	0.2855	0.0264	0.2052	0.1300	0.0044
2b	0.4732	0.1156	0.0563	0.0230	0.0983	0.4958	0.1355	0.0496	0.0282	0.0959	0.4707	0.0949	0.0475	0.0078	0.1643
2c	0.2386	0.0033	0.3037	0.0119	0.1185	0.2659	0.0041	0.1789	0.1025	0.1659	0.1189	0.1474	0.3614	0.0124	0.0026
2d	0.0538	0.2794	0.0019	0.0091	0.4613	0.0391	0.1876	0.0249	0.0287	0.5506	0.1543	0.2490	0.0030	0.0054	0.1891
2e	0.2134	0.1082	0.1658	0.0276	0.0521	0.1374	0.1119	0.2976	0.0316	0.0087	0.4977	0.0008	0.0549	0.0024	0.0797
2f	0.2671	0.3953	0.0449	0.0588	0.0251	0.3358	0.3694	0.0035	0.1065	0.0064	0.0482	0.3960	0.2045	0.0172	0.0566
2g	0.0399	0.0217	0.0252	0.8482	0.0056	0.0434	0.0203	0.0934	0.6747	0.0582	0.0529	0.0448	0.0228	0.7991	0.0030
2h	0.3230	0.3174	0.0180	0.0260	0.1107	0.3801	0.3127	0.0073	0.0151	0.0949	0.0626	0.5028	0.1026	0.0001	0.2204
2i	0.1904	0.0039	0.2062	0.0085	0.0151	0.1849	0.0001	0.1250	0.0390	0.0002	0.1707	0.0768	0.2623	0.0174	0.1347
D3	0.9732	0.0239				0.9779	0.0208				0.9819	0.0139			
3a	0.6479	0.0002	0.0007	0.0001		0.6874	0.0031	0.0016	0.0020		0.4432	0.1661	0.0082	0.1407	
3b	0.6477	0.0007	0.0002	0.0002		0.6919	0.0001	0.0000	0.0003		0.4348	0.1828	0.0013	0.1181	
3c	0.0010	0.0664	0.9155	0.0170		0.0007	0.2017	0.5458	0.2516		0.0095	0.0013	0.9864	0.0002	
3d	0.0005	0.4865	0.0078	0.5050		0.0051	0.5089	0.0021	0.4830		0.1674	0.4448	0.0005	0.2615	
3e	0.0000	0.4560	0.0752	0.4687		0.0006	0.2904	0.4516	0.2569		0.1951	0.4127	0.0024	0.2730	

*indicators 1a to 3e refer to Table 4. D1=dimension *Access*, D2=dimension *Products*, D3=dimension *Soundness*.
Source: Calculations based on administrative enterprise data from Credit Bureau Cambodia, 2019.

Table 18: Weights for Index, Finance Sub-Index (Financial Depth), Cambodia

I. Financial depth			All		MSMEs		Large firms	
Dimension 1 –Access			Weights	0.3330	Weights	0.3332	Weights	0.3328
1a	Bank loans outstanding from state-owned banks –total	value	0.2186		0.2026		0.2269	
1b	Bank loans outstanding from private sector banks –LCY	value	0.1979		0.1973		0.1992	
1c	Bank loans outstanding from private sector banks –FCY	value	0.2175		0.2026		0.2219	
1d	Loans from microfinance institutions –LCY	value	0.2016		0.1988		0.2072	
1e	Loans from microfinance institutions –FCY	value	0.1644		0.1986		0.1447	
Dimension 2 –Products			Weights	0.3340	Weights	0.3336	Weights	0.3343
2a	No collateral	dummy	0.1165		0.1208		0.1001	
2b	Immovable assets	dummy	0.1174		0.1218		0.1206	
2c	Movable assets	dummy	0.1036		0.1085		0.0987	
2d	Corporate guarantees	dummy	0.1234		0.1257		0.0923	
2e	Other collaterals	dummy	0.0869		0.0888		0.0976	
2f	Loan purpose –working capital	dummy	0.1212		0.1243		0.1110	
2g	Loan purpose –investment capital	dummy	0.1441		0.1347		0.1417	
2h	Loan purpose –others	dummy	0.1218		0.1225		0.1365	
2i	Loan tenor –average	category	0.0650		0.0528		0.1017	
Dimension 3 –Soundness			Weights	0.3330	Weights	0.3332	Weights	0.3329
3a	Overdue loans (performing loans) –LCY	value	0.1510		0.1583		0.1784	
3b	Overdue loans (performing loans) –FCY	value	0.1510		0.1579		0.1734	
3c	Overdue loans (nonperforming loans) –LCY	value	0.2327		0.2280		0.2347	
3d	Overdue loans (nonperforming loans) –FCY	value	0.2326		0.2279		0.2057	
3e	Overdue loans (write-off) –total	value	0.2327		0.2280		0.2078	
Overall				1.0000		1.0000		1.0000

FCY = foreign currency; LCY = local currency; MSME = micro, small, and medium-sized enterprise.
Note: number of observations: (all) 1,344, (MSMEs) 1,029, (large firms) 315.
Source: Calculations based on administrative enterprise data from Credit Bureau Cambodia, 2019.

Second-Stage Principal Component Analysis

Referring to Table 16, eigenvalues in the overall dimension were calculated as the aggregation of three dimensions (*Access, Products, and Soundness*). As the first two components accounted for 99.9% of the variance and had eigenvalues of 0.95 or higher, we used these two components for the second-stage PCA. Similar to the first-stage PCA, squared loadings were calculated in two components (Z_1 and Z_2) (Table 17). Then, weights were obtained in each dimension, *Access, Products, and Soundness*, following the same path of analysis as in the first-stage PCA (Table 18).

The result (Figure 4) highlights that each dimension has almost equal weight (score); that is, MSME access to finance, products in MSME financing, and overdue conditions equally impact the level of MSME financial depth. For the dimension *Access* (D1), we could see that loans from state-owned banks and USD-denominated loans from private sector banks support MSME access to finance (figures marked in yellow). For the dimension *Products* (D2), immovable assets and corporate guarantees have a relatively significant role in financing MSMEs. Lending to MSMEs also facilitates their investment capital financing (slightly higher than working capital financing). For the dimension *Soundness* (D3), NPLs in both local currency and USD-denominated loans are relatively higher for MSMEs (even compared with large firms).

Overall, MSMEs' financial depth can be highly affected by loans from state-owned banks and USD-denominated loans from private sector banks, backed by immovable assets (land) as collateral and corporate guarantees, which support their access to investment capital financing. Meanwhile, financing MSMEs holds relatively higher risk than financing large firms. NBFIs have relatively less contribution to MSME access to finance. This suggests that, to increase the financial depth of MSMEs, the diversification of financing options for MSMEs beyond traditional bank lending is needed, which involves well-organized risk management for loans as well as reconsidering the role of state-owned banks.

Figure 4: Financial Depth Dimension of the Finance Sub-Index, Cambodia

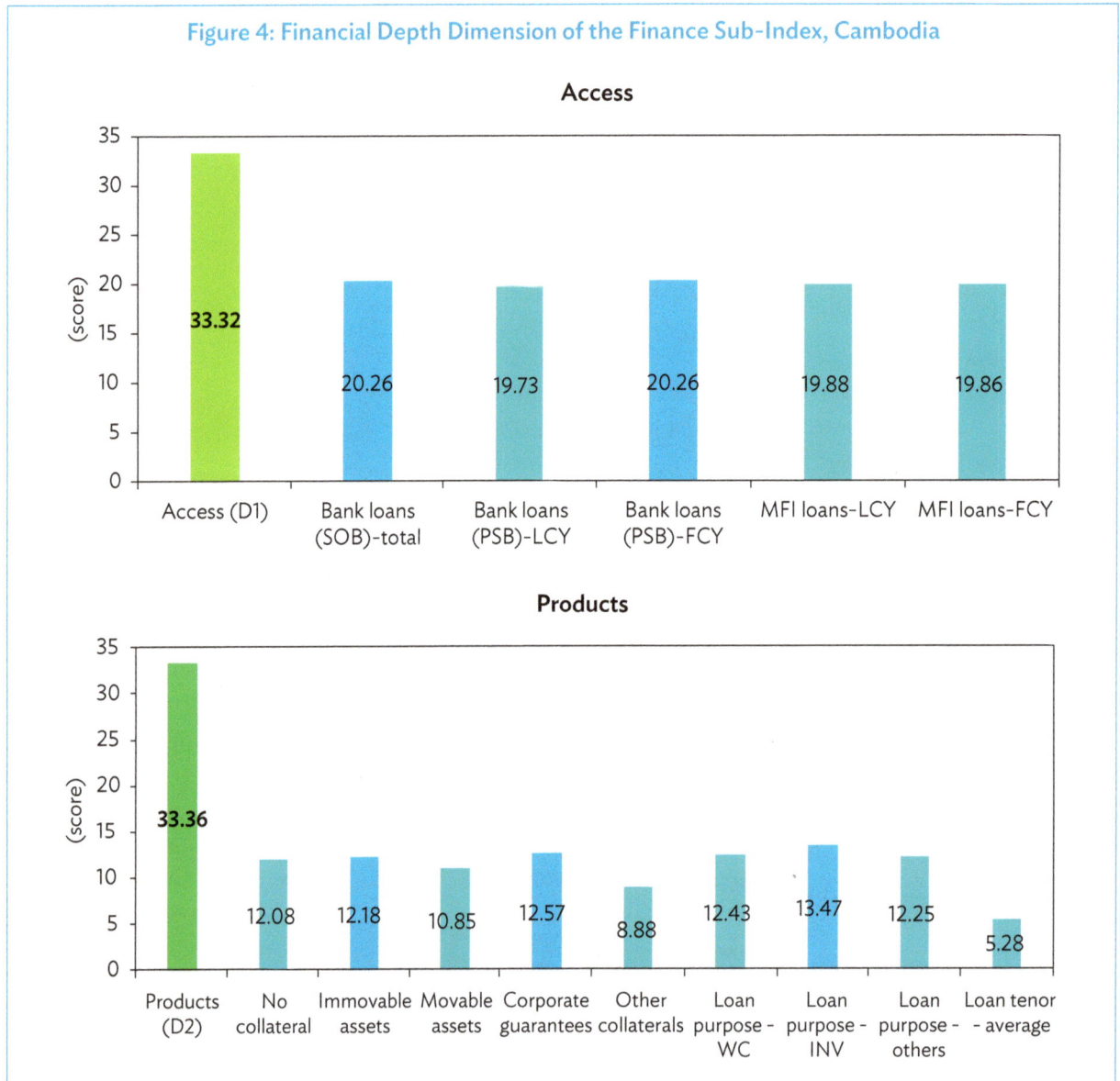

Access

Products

continued on next page

Figure 4 continued

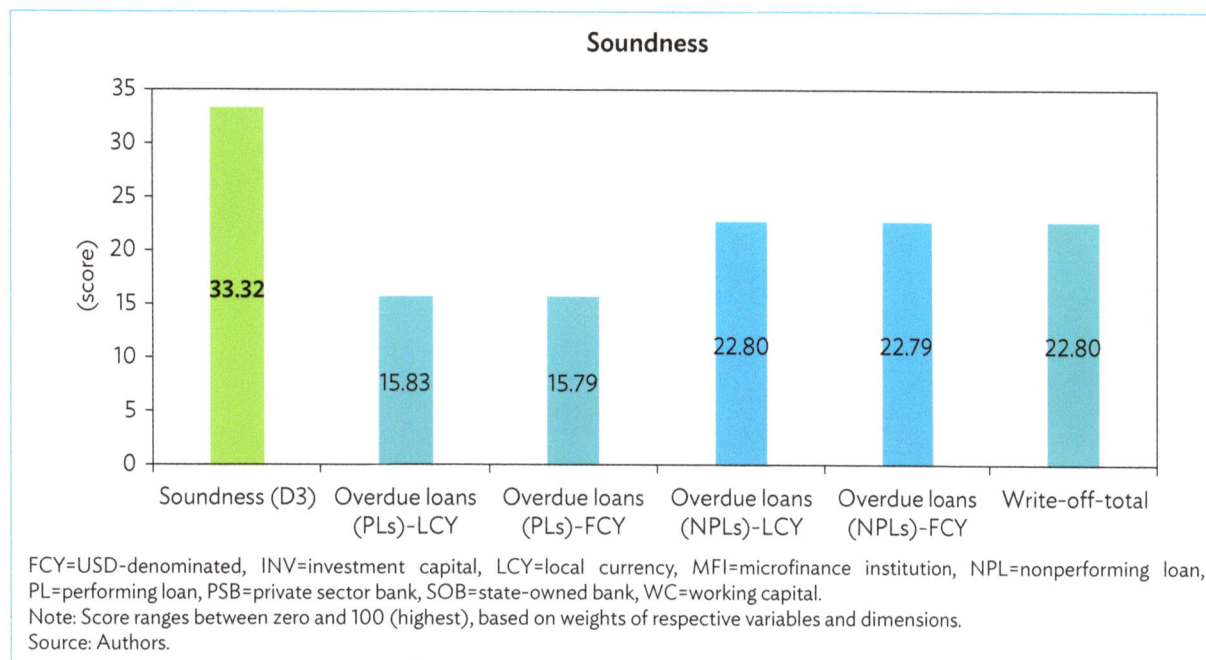

Soundness

FCY=USD-denominated, INV=investment capital, LCY=local currency, MFI=microfinance institution, NPL=nonperforming loan, PL=performing loan, PSB=private sector bank, SOB=state-owned bank, WC=working capital.
Note: Score ranges between zero and 100 (highest), based on weights of respective variables and dimensions.
Source: Authors.

3.   Challenges for Designing an SME Development Index

There are two notable challenges in designing the SME-DI. The first is **data availability**. Data collection of MSME activity, particularly operations and access to finance, remains nascent in several Southeast Asian countries that ADB serves. It refers to data availability (Table 5) and the number of categories where data are not available. Although data collection has generally improved since the previous ASM in 2014, there are still gaps.

In some instances, the issue is that only a few organizations collect the desired information, and more resources need to be devoted to the task. In other instances, the barrier is that while data are collected, it is not made public or otherwise shared. This can occur both with government agencies and with private actors such as credit bureaus. More data-sharing arrangements with statistics offices, government authorities, central banks, and other financial authorities can help.

A second obstacle is **data consistency**. This can be of two kinds: (i) within country, such as a standard definition of MSMEs among various actors such as government ministries, banks, and NBFIs; and (ii) across countries. For the former, several countries use different MSME definitions depending upon industrial sector—whether agriculture, manufacturing, or services—as well as different definitions based on loan size and/or listing requirements on stock exchanges. For example, in Cambodia, the national definition of an MSME differentiates by sector, yet ACLEDA, the largest commercial bank, characterizes a small business loan as any borrowing up to $50,000, and a medium-sized enterprise loan as a loan from $50,000 to $1 million.[15]

Across countries, there are similar issues regarding MSME definitions and other classifications. For example, loan terms (short, medium, or long) vary depending on national context. The CBC uses 1–12 months for short term, 13–59 months for medium term, and 60+ months for long term, but this is by no means standard across Asia, or

---

[15]   Asia Small and Medium-Sized Enterprise Monitor 2020 Volume 1-Country and Regional Reviews, p.79.

even Southeast Asia. The Lao Development Bank issues loans for a maximum 60 months. Aggregating data, even when available, therefore becomes a challenge without consistency. One remedy would be to conduct focused, specific national surveys, where questions can be standardized ahead of data collection. We intend to pursue this in future versions of the SME-DI.

Conclusion

The purpose of this technical note is to present the initial design of the new SME-DI. We started with an overview of the MSME landscape in Southeast Asia. We then provided a synopsis of existing global data initiatives for MSMEs, and reviewed the relevant academic literature for index development. We next described our data and its selection, as well as the empirical approach used for analysis: the two-stage PCA.

Our data consists of two distinct sets: aggregate national-level time series data for the regional index and granular firm-level data for the country index. For aggregate data, we estimated the SME-DI using three dimensions (Macro, Bank, Nonbank) and four dimensions (the prior three plus Equity). The former is more plausible given our current data, while the latter represents our future direction given the importance of equity financing for MSMEs. What we learned from our analysis is that the macro conditions are the most significant factors for MSME development. MSME financing remains important; the weights for Bank and Nonbank are almost equal. Policymakers need to pay attention to both financing sectors, though their approach to each will likely differ. Accessing finance from banks may require more financial literacy training for MSMEs to increase their success rate in obtaining bank loans. On the other hand, MSMEs generally find it easier to access finance from NBFIs, so further developing this sector is advisable.

The second analysis yielded initial findings from the test-run of the two-stage PCA, based on only CBC administrative enterprise data. The result shows the estimated scores of the financial depth dimension under the Finance Sub-Index at the national level. In terms of financial access, products, and soundness, the result suggests that loans from state-owned banks and USD-denominated loans from private sector banks, with real estate security and corporate guarantees, positively affect MSME financial depth, supporting their access to investment capital financing. Financing MSMEs holds relatively higher risks than financing large firms. The nonbank finance industry represented by MFIs contributed relatively less to MSME access to finance, suggesting that more diversified financing options for MSMEs are needed. To increase MSME financial depth, more structured risk management for MSME loans is required along with rethinking the role of state-owned banks.

CBC's enterprise data cover 1,029 MSMEs registered with CBC—far less than the MSME total in Cambodia. The analytical model on the financial depth dimension can be improved further, together with additional analysis using consumer data of around 20,000 that address business loans by self-employed and sole proprietorships. In that analysis, we will consider some factors we did not use in this test-run—such as location, operating period, and business sector—to improve the financial depth model.

The notable challenges in designing the SME-DI are data availability and consistency. Southeast Asia has relatively better data availability on MSMEs than other regions in developing Asia. Nevertheless, many data remain missing if we are to fully estimate the SME-DI. Further efforts are required to obtain country data through (i) extended data-sharing agreements with public and private sector institutions that hold MSME data—including statistics offices, business registration offices, credit bureaus, government authorities, financial authorities, and central banks—and (ii) dedicated national firm-level surveys to fill in missing data.

Moving forward, we will strengthen the MSME database through the ASM project with necessary stakeholder surveys and aim for more granular firm-level data through strengthened data-sharing agreements with MSME data-holding institutions—to continue to design and develop the SME-DI based on our conceptual framework. For the next step, we will test other analytical options such as dynamic factor modeling (DFM) and principal component pursuit (PCP), with supplementary analysis using ordinary least squares (OLS) and qualitative scoring methods.

References

Asian Development Bank (ADB). 2020a. Asia Small and Medium-Sized Enterprise Monitor 2020: Volume I–Country and Regional Reviews. Manila.

ADB. 2020b. Asia Small and Medium-Sized Enterprise Monitor 2020: Volume II–COVID-19 Impact on Micro, Small, and Medium-Sized Enterprises in Developing Asia. Manila.

Asia Professional Education Network (APEN). 2017. *JAIF Project: Comprehensive Industrial Human Resource Development (Ci-HRD) Project: Final Report (Part I)*. Tokyo.

Abeyasekera, Savitri. 2005. Multivariate Methods for Index Construction. In *Household Sample Surveys in Developing and Transition Economies:* Chapter 18: 367-388. United Nations Department of Economic and Social Affairs, Statistics Division. New York.

Adelman, Irma and Cynthia Taft Morris. 1973. *Economic Growth and Social Equity in Developing Countries*. Stanford: Stanford University Press.

Bo, Chen and Yuen Pau Woo. 2008. *A Composite Index of Economic Integration in the Asia-Pacific Region*. New York: United Nations Public Administration Network.

Bouwmans, Thierry and El Hadi Zahzah. 2014. "Robust PCA via Principal Component Pursuit: A Review for a Comparative Evaluation in Video Surveillance." *Computer Vision and Image Understanding 122*: 22-34.

Candes, Emanuel Jean, Xiaodong Li, Yi Ma, and John Wright. 2009. "Robust Principal Component Analysis?" https://arxiv.org/pdf/0912.3599.pdf (accessed August 2019)

Debuque-Gonzales, Margarita and Maria Socorro Gochoco-Bautista. 2013. Financial Conditions Indexes for Asian Economies. *ADB Economics Working Papers Series* No. 333.

Economic Research Institute for ASEAN and East Asia (ERIA) and Organisation for Economic Co-operation and Development (OECD). 2014. ASEAN *SME Policy Index 2014: Towards Competitive and Innovative ASEAN SMEs*. Jakarta.

Federici, Alessandro and Andrea Mazzitelli. 2005. "Dynamic Factor Analysis with STATA." 2nd Italian STATA Users Group Meeting: Milan, Italy.

Gygli, Savina, Florian Haelg, and Jan-Egbert Sturm. 2018. "The KOF Globalisation Index-Revisited." *KOF Working Paper 439*.

Huh, Hyeon-Seung, and Cyn-Young Park. 2017. "Asia-Pacific Regional Integration Index: Construction, Interpretation, and Comparison." *ADB Economics Working Papers Series* No. 511. https://www.adb.org/publications/asia-pacific-regional-integration-index.

International Finance Corporation. 2017. *MSME Finance Gap*. Washington, DC.

International Trade Centre. 2019. *SME Competitiveness Outlook 2019*. Geneva.

OECD. 2019. *OECD SME and Entrepreneurship Outlook 2019*. Paris: OECD Publishing.

OECD. 2020. *Financing SMEs and Entrepreneurs 2020: An OECD Scoreboard*. Paris: OECD Publishing.

OECD and ERIA. 2018. *SME Policy Index: ASEAN 2018*. Paris: OECD Publishing.

Park, Cyn-Young and Racquel Claveria. 2018. Constructing the Asia-Pacific Regional Cooperation and Integration Index: A Panel Approach. *ADB Economics Working Papers Series*. No. 544. Manila: ADB.

Shigehiro, Shinozaki. 2014. "A New Regime of SME Finance in Emerging Asia: Enhancing Access to Growth Capital and Policy Implications". *Journal of International Commerce, Economics and Policy*. Vol. 5, No. 3. World Scientific Publishing.

Shaukat, S. Shahid, Toqeer Ahmed Rao, and Moazzam A. Khan. 2016. "Impact of Sample Size on Principal Component Analysis Ordination of an Environmental Data Set: Effects on Eigenstructure." *Ekologia (Bratislavia) 35* (2): 173-190.

Stock, James Harold and Mark W. Watson. 2010. Dynamic Factor Models. In M.P. Clements and D.F. Henry, eds. *Oxford Handbook of Economic Forecasting*. Oxford: Oxford University Press.

World Bank. The LPI Methodology. https://wb-lpi-media.s3.amazonaws.com/LPI%20Methodology.pdf (accessed August 2019).

Annex: Profile of Cambodian Enterprises

A. Location

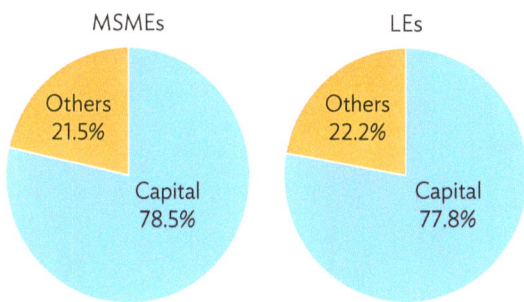

B. Company Age

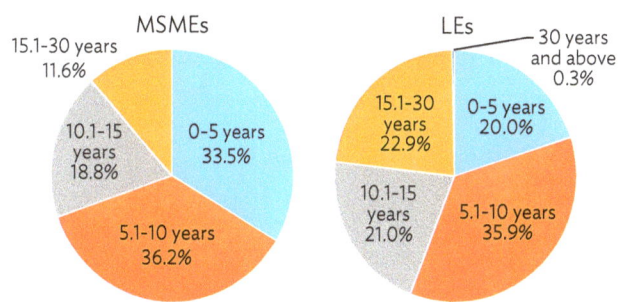

C. Business Sector

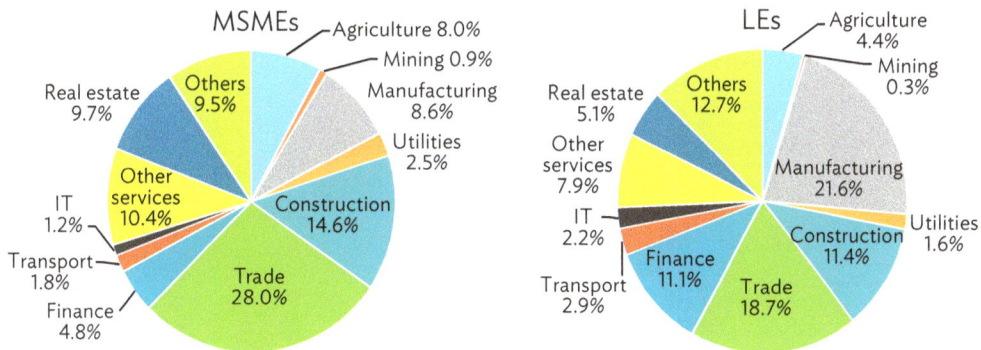

D. Employment

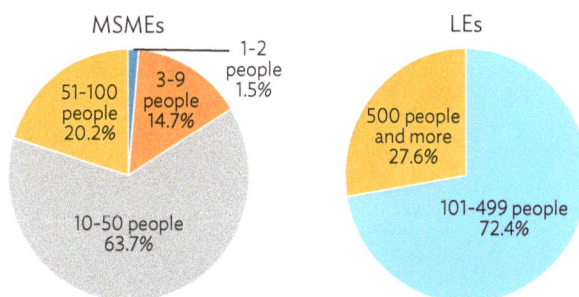

E-1. Loans Outstanding, Average

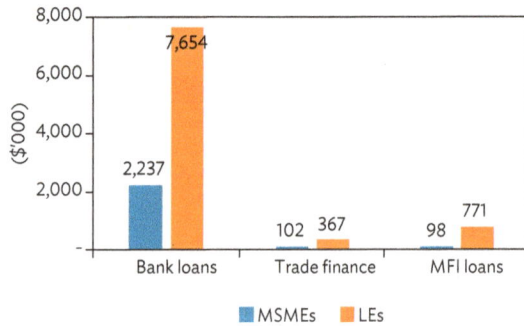

E-2. Loan Purpose

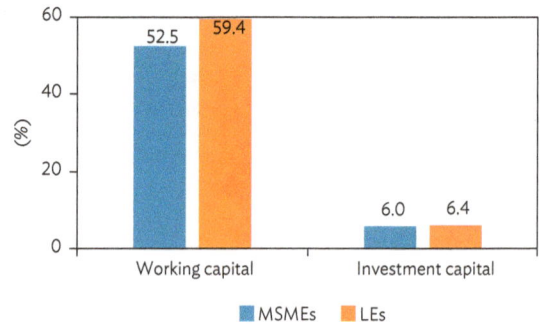

E-3. Loan Tenor, Average

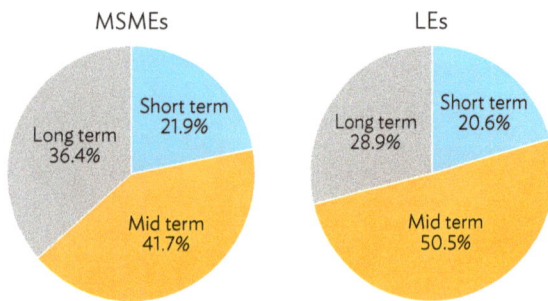

E-4. Collateral and Guarantees

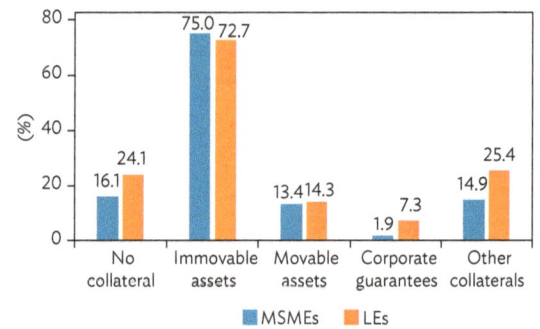

E-5. Overdue Conditions

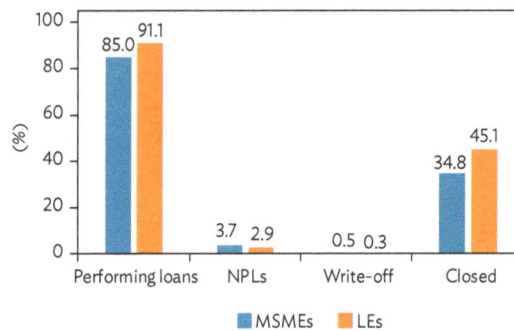

LE = large enterprise; MFI = microfinance institution; MSME = micro, small, and medium-sized enterprise; NPL = nonperforming loan.
Source: Calculated based on Credit Bureau Cambodia data, 2019.